CAVENDIS

Business Law

Third Edition

Cavendish
Publishing
Limited

London • Sydney • Portland, Oregon

Third edition first published in Great Britain 2004 by
Cavendish Publishing Limited, The Glass House,
Wharton Street, London WC1X 9PX, United Kingdom
Telephone: + 44 (0)20 7278 8000   Facsimile: + 44 (0)20 7278 8080
Email: info@cavendishpublishing.com
Website: www.cavendishpublishing.com

Published in the United States by Cavendish Publishing
c/o International Specialized Book Services,
5824 NE Hassalo Street, Portland,
Oregon 97213-3644, USA

Published in Australia by Cavendish Publishing (Australia) Pty Ltd
45 Beach Street, Coogee, NSW 2034, Australia

Cataloguing in Publication Data
Data available

ISBN 1-85941-875-9

1 3 5 7 9 10 8 6 4 2

Typeset by Phoenix Photosetting, Chatham, Kent
Printed and bound in Great Britain

Contents

1 Sources of law

Legislation: law produced by Parliament

There are five stages, in each House of Parliament (Commons and Lords), through which a Bill must pass in order to become law:

- first reading;
- second reading;
- committee stage;
- report stage;
- third reading.

Then it is given royal assent. The House of Lords has limited scope to delay legislation.

Delegated legislation: power delegated by Parliament to others to make law

Types of delegated legislation include:

- Orders in Council;
- statutory instruments;
- bylaws;
- professional regulations.

Advantages	Speed of implementation Saving of parliamentary time. Access to expertise; flexibility.
Disadvantages	Lack of accountability. Lack of scrutiny. Lack of public knowledge.

Controls

Parliament   Joint Select Committee on Statutory Instruments.

Courts   *Ultra vires* provisions may be challenged through judicial review.

Ultra vires means that the party to whom power was delegated has exceeded its authority.

Case law

Law created by judges in the course of deciding cases.

Stare decisis

Binding precedent: courts are bound by the previous decisions of courts equal or above them in the court hierarchy (see below, p 4).

Ratio decidendi	The legal reason for decision binds.
Overruling	The case is said to be different from precedent, therefore it does not have to be followed.
Obiter dictum	Anything not in *ratio* does not have to be followed.
Distinguishing	A court higher up in the hierarchy sets aside a legal ruling established in a previous case.

The House of Lords can overrule its previous decisions (*Practice Statement* (1966)); lower courts, including the Court of Appeal, cannot, except in special circumstances (*Young v Bristol Aeroplane Co Ltd* (1944)).

Advantages	Time-saving. Certainty. Flexibility.
Disadvantages	Unconstitutionality. Uncertainty. Fixity.

NB: notice the contradictory nature of the advantages and disadvantages.

Court structure

Civil   *Criminal*

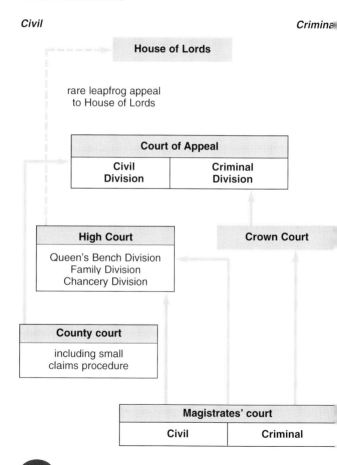

House of Lords

rare leapfrog appeal
to House of Lords

Court of Appeal	
Civil Division	**Criminal Division**

High Court
Queen's Bench Division
Family Division
Chancery Division

Crown Court

County court
including small claims procedure

Magistrates' court	
Civil	**Criminal**

Statutory interpretation: how judges give practical meaning to legislation

The rules of interpretation

- *The literal rule*: gives words in legislation their everyday meaning, even if this leads to an apparent injustice (*Fisher v Bell* (1961)).
- *The golden rule*: used where the literal rule will result in an obvious absurdity (*Adler v George* (1964)).
- *The mischief rule*: permits the court to go beyond the words of the statute in question to consider the mischief at which it was aimed (*Corkery v Carpenter* (1950)).

Influenced by the European Court of Justice, UK courts are increasingly adopting a purposive approach when interpreting statute. In practice this often has a similar effect to the application of the mischief rule.

Intrinsic assistance	Relies on the internal evidence of the statute: its title, preamble, or schedules.
Extrinsic assistance	Goes beyond the Act to dictionaries, textbooks, other statutes including the Interpretation Act, reports, other parliamentary papers.

Aids to construction

Since *Pepper v Hart* (1993), *Hansard* may also be consulted.

Presumptions in interpreting statutes

Unless expressly rebutted, the following presumptions apply

Against	Alteration of the common law.
	Retrospective application.
	Deprivation of an individual's liberty, property or rights.
	Retrospective application.
	Application to the Crown.
In favour of	Requirement for *mens rea* in criminal offences.
	Deriving the meaning of words from their contexts – the *noscitur a sociis* rule, the *eiusdem generis rule*, and the *expressio unius exclusio alterius* rule.

2 European Union law

Sources

Treaties

Internal treaties	Eg the Treaty of Rome. Govern the Member States of the Union and anything contained therein supersedes domestic legal provisions.
International treaties	Negotiated by the European Commission on behalf of the Union. Binding on the members of the Union.

Secondary legislation

Regulations	Apply without the need for Member States to pass their own legislation.
Directives	State general goals and leave the Member States to implement them. The European Court of Justice can enforce Directives.
Decisions	Commission Decisions on the operation of European laws have the force of law under Art 249 EC Treaty (formerly Art 189).

Judgments of the European Court of Justice

Overrule those of national courts or national legislation.

The institutions of the European Union

➲ *The Council of Ministers* is made up of ministerial representatives from each of the 15 Member States of the EU and is the supreme decision making body of the EU. Qualified majority voting is the procedure in which the votes of the 15 Member States are weighted in proportion to their population, from 10 down to two votes each.

⊃ *The European Parliament* is directly elected. There are a total of 626 members (87 from the UK), divided amongst the 15 Member States approximately in proportion to the size of their various populations.

It is a consultative, rather than a legislative, institution and is subsidiary to the Council of Ministers.

⊃ *The Commission* is the executive of the European Union. There are 20 Commissioners chosen from the Member States. The Maastricht Treaty extended the term of office from four to five years; this is renewable. Commissioners have specific responsibility for particular areas of Union policy. The Commission is responsible for ensuring that Treaty obligations and Regulations are met. It has been given wide powers to investigate and punish breaches of EU Law.

⊃ *The Court of Justice* is the judicial arm of the EU in the field of EU law, and its judgments overrule those of national courts. It decides whether any measures adopted by the Commission, Council or any national government are compatible with Treaty obligations.

It also provides authoritative rulings, at the request of national courts, under Art 234 (formerly Art 177) of the EC Treaty, on the interpretation of points of EU law. See *Factortame Ltd v Secretary of State for Transport* (1989) and (1991).

3 Alternative dispute resolution

Arbitration

This is the procedure whereby parties in dispute refer the issue to a third party for resolution, rather than take the case to the ordinary law courts.

Arbitration procedures can be contained in the original contract or agreed after a dispute arises.

The procedure is governed by the Arbitration Act 1996, which reflects a shift from judicial control to the parties themselves deciding how they want their dispute resolved.

Arbitrators

Under the Act, arbitrators have a general duty to act fairly and impartially between the parties, giving each a reasonable opportunity to state its case; and to adopt procedures suitable for the circumstance of the case, thereby avoiding unnecessary delay or expense.

Arbitrators must decide the dispute:

- in accordance with the law chosen by the parties; or
- in accordance with such other considerations as the parties have agreed.

The court

The court has power, under s 24, to revoke the appointment of an arbitrator where the arbitrator has not acted impartially; does not possess the required qualifications; does not have either the physical or mental capacity to deal with the proceedings; or has failed to conduct the proceedings properly.

Once the decision of the panel has been made, there are limited grounds for appeal to the court in relation to:

- the substantive jurisdiction of the panel;
- procedural grounds;
- a point of law.

Where the parties agree to the arbitral panel making a decision without providing a reasoned justification for it, they will also lose the right to appeal.

Advantages over ordinary court system

The advantages of arbitration may be summarised as follows:

- privacy;
- informality;
- speed;
- lower cost;
- expertise;
- less antagonistic.

Small claims procedure in the county court is a distinct process, despite being referred to as arbitration.

Tribunals

As an alternative to the court system, a large number of tribunals have been set up under various Acts of Parliament to rule on the operation of the particular schemes established under those Acts.

Over a quarter of a million cases are dealt with by tribunals each year.

Administrative tribunals	Deal with cases involving conflicts between the State, its functionaries and private citizens.
Domestic tribunals	Deal with private internal matters within institutions.

Tribunals may be administrative, but they are also adjudicative, in that they have to act judicially when deciding particular cases.

Tribunals are subject to the supervision of the Council on Tribunals, but are also under the control of the ordinary courts.

Tribunals usually comprise three members, only one of whom, the chair, is expected to be legally qualified.

Examples of tribunals

Examples of tribunals include:

- employment tribunals;
- Social Security Appeals Tribunal;
- Mental Health Review Tribunal;
- Lands Tribunal;
- Rent Assessment Committee.

Advantages	Speed and cost. Informality and flexibility. Expertise. Accessibility. Privacy.
Disadvantages	Appeals procedure. Lack of publicity. Lack of legal aid in most cases.

Mediation and conciliation

◯ *Mediation* is the process whereby a third party acts as the conduit through which two disputing parties communicate and negotiate in an attempt to reach a common resolution of a problem.

◯ *Conciliation* gives the mediator the power to suggest grounds for compromise and the possible basis for a conclusive agreement.

Both mediation and conciliation have been available in relation to industrial disputes under the auspices of the government funded Advisory, Conciliation and Arbitration Service (ACAS).

Advantage	The parties to the dispute determine their own solutions and therefore feel committed to the outcome.
Disadvantages	Mediation has no binding power and does not always lead to an outcome. Mediation does not necessarily challenge inherent power differentials in relationships.

4 Contract

The formation of contracts

The essential elements of a binding contractual agreement are as follows:

- offer;
- acceptance;
- consideration;
- capacity;
- intention to create legal relations;
- no vitiating factors.

The first five of these elements must be present, and the sixth absent.

Offer

An offer is a promise, which is capable of acceptance, to be bound on particular terms.

An offer must be distinguished from the following:

- a mere statement of intention (*Kleinwort Benson v Malaysian Mining Corp* (1989));
- a mere supply of information (*Harvey v Facey* (1893));
- an invitation to treat. This is an invitation to others to make offers. An invitation to treat cannot be accepted in such a way as to form a contract, nor can the person extending the invitation be bound to accept any offers made to them. Examples of invitations to treat are:
  - the display of goods in a shop window (*Fisher v Bell* (1961));

- the display of goods on the shelf of a self-service shop (*Pharmaceutical Society of Great Britain v Boots Cash Chemists* (1953));
- a public advertisement (*Partridge v Crittenden* (1968));
- a share prospectus: contrary to common understanding, such a document is merely an invitation to treat, inviting people to make offers to subscribe for shares in a company;
- auctions operate on the basis of the auctioneer inviting, and accepting offers from the bidders.

Offers to particular people

An offer may be made to a particular person, to a group of people, or to the world at large. In the latter case, it can be accepted by anyone (*Carlill v Carbolic Smoke Ball Co* (1893)).

Termination of offers

If an offer is accepted (see below), a contract is formed, but the offer can be brought to an end without involving the creation of a contract, as follows:

- *rejection*: if a person to whom an offer has been made rejects it, then they cannot subsequently accept the original offer;
- *a counter-offer*: where the offeree tries to change the terms of the original offer, they cannot then accept the terms of the original offer (*Hyde v Wrench* (1840));
- a counter-offer should not be confused with a *request for information*, which does not end the offer (*Stevenson v McLean* (1880));
- *revocation of offer*: where the offeror withdraws the offer, means that the offer cannot be accepted (*Routledge v Grant* (1828)). Revocation must be received by the

offeree, but communication may be made through a reliable third party (*Dickinson v Dodds* (1876));

- where *an option contract* has been created, the offeror cannot withdraw the offer before the agreed time. In the case of unilateral contracts, revocation is not permissible once the offeree has started performing the task requested (*Errington v Errington* (1952));

- *lapse of offers*: occurs where the parties agree, or the offeror sets, a time limit within which acceptance has to take place. If the offer is not accepted within that period, then it lapses and can no longer be accepted. Where no time limit has been set, it will still lapse after a reasonable time, depending on the circumstances of the case.

Acceptance

Acceptance of an offer creates a contract, but acceptance must correspond with the terms of the offer. Remember the following:

- *knowledge and motive*: no one can accept an offer that they do not know about, but the motive for accepting is not important (*Williams v Carwadine* (1883));

- *form of acceptance*: acceptance may be in the form of express words, either spoken or written; but, equally, it may be implied from conduct (*Brogden v Metropolitan Railway Co* (1877));

- *communication of acceptance*: acceptance must be communicated to the offeror: silence cannot amount to acceptance (*Felthouse v Bindley* (1863));
  except:
  - in unilateral contracts (*Carlill v Carbolic Smoke Ball Co* (1893));

- where the postal rule operates (*Adams v Lindsell* (1818)). The postal rule applies to telegrams: it does not apply to instantaneous communication (*Entores v Far East Corp* (1955)).

The postal rule only applies where the parties expect the post to be used as the means of acceptance. It can be excluded by explicitly requiring that acceptance is only to be effective on receipt (see *Holwell Securities v Hughes* (1974)).

Consideration

In *Dunlop v Selfridge* (1915), the House of Lords adopted the following definition of consideration:

> An act or forbearance of one party, or the promise thereof, is the price for which the promise of the other is bought, and the promise thus given for value is enforceable.

Types of consideration

Executory consideration

This is the promise to perform an action at some future time. A contract can thus be made on the basis of an exchange of promises as to future action.

Executed consideration

In the case of unilateral contracts, where the offeror promises something in return for the offeree's doing something, the promise only becomes enforceable when the offeree has actually performed the required act.

Past consideration

This category does not actually count as consideration. With past consideration, the action is performed before the promise that it is supposed to be the consideration for. Such action is not sufficient to support a later promise (*Re McArdle* (1951)).

There are exceptions to the rule that past consideration will not support a valid contract:

- under s 27 of the Bills of Exchange Act 1882;
- under s 29 of the Limitation Act 1980, a time barred debt becomes enforceable again if it is acknowledged in writing;
- where the claimant performed the action at the request of the defendant and payment was expected (*Re Casey's Patents* (1892)).

Rules relating to consideration

To be effective, consideration must comply with certain rules:

- consideration must not be past (see above);
- performance must be legal;
- performance must be possible;
- consideration must move from the promisee (*Tweddle v Atkinson* (1861));
- consideration must be sufficient, but need not be adequate: the court will not intervene to require equality in the value exchanged, as long as the agreement has been freely entered into (*Thomas v Thomas* (1842); *Chappell and Co v Nestle Co* (1959)).

Performance of existing duties

There are rules regarding performance of existing duties:

- performance of a public duty cannot be consideration for a promised reward (*Collins v Godefroy* (1831)). Where a promisee does more than his/her duty, the or she is entitled to claim on the promise (*Glassbrook v Glamorgan CC* (1925));

⬭ performance of a contractual duty: the rule used to be that the performance of an existing contractual duty owed to the promisor could not be consideration for a new promise (see *Stilk v Myrick* (1809)). Some additional consideration had to be provided (see *Hartley v Ponsonby* (1857)). *Williams v Roffey Bros* (1990) now appears to allow performance of an existing contractual duty to provide consideration for a new promise in circumstances where there is no question of fraud or duress, and where the promisor receives practical benefits;

⬭ performance of a contractual duty owed to one person can amount to valid consideration for the promise made by another person (see *Shadwell v Shadwell* (1860)).

Consideration in relation to the waiver of existing rights

In *Pinnel's Case* (1602), it was stated that a payment of a lesser sum cannot be any satisfaction for the whole. This opinion was approved in *Foakes v Beer* (1884).

However, the following will operate to discharge an outstanding debt fully:

⬭ payment in kind;
⬭ payment at a different place;
⬭ payment of a lesser sum by a third party;
⬭ a composition arrangement between creditors that they will accept part payment of their debts;
⬭ estoppel: see below.

Promissory estoppel

This equitable doctrine prevents promisors from going back on their promises. The doctrine first appeared in *Hughes v Metropolitan Railway Co* (1877) and was revived in *Central London Property Trust Ltd v High Trees House Ltd* (1947).

The precise scope of the doctrine of promissory estoppel is far from certain. However, the following points may be made:

- it arises from a promise made by a party to an existing contractual agreement (*WJ Alan and Co v El Nasr Export and Import Co* (1972));
- it only varies or discharges of rights within a contract, and does not apply to the formation of contracts;
- it normally only suspends rights (*Tool Metal Manufacturing Co v Tungsten Electric Co* (1955));
- rights may be extinguished, however, in the case of a non-continuing obligation, or where the parties cannot resume their original positions;
- the promise relied upon must be given voluntarily (*D and C Builders v Rees* (1966)).

Capacity

Capacity refers to a person's ability to enter into a contract. In general, all adults of sound mind have full capacity. The capacity of certain individuals, however, is limited by the Minors' Contracts Act 1987.

Minors

A minor is a person under the age of 18 (the age of majority was reduced from 21 to 18 by the Family Reform Act 1969). The law tries to protect such persons by restricting their contractual capacity and thus preventing them from entering into disadvantageous agreements.

Agreements entered into by minors may be classified within three possible categories:

Valid contracts	Voidable contracts	Unenforceable contracts
Enforceable against minors. Contracts for necessaries: necessaries are goods suitable to the condition in life of the minor and their actual requirements at the time of sale (s 3 of the Sale of Goods Act 1979; *Nash v Inman* (1908)).	Enforceable against minors, unless repudiated during minority, or a reasonable time thereafter. Transactions involving continuing obligations, eg contracts for shares, or leases of property, or partnership agreements.	Unenforceable against minors; absolutely void under the Infants Relief Act 1874. Contracts for the repayment of loans; contracts for goods other than necessaries; accounts stated, ie admissions of money owed.
Beneficial contracts of service: a minor is bound by a contract of apprenticeship or employment, as long as it is, on the whole, for their benefit (*Doyle v White City Stadium* (1935)). There has to be an element of education or training in the contract and ordinary trading contracts will not be enforced (*Mercantile Union Guarantee Corpn v Ball* (1937)).	Payments made prior to repudiation: cannot be recovered unless there is a total failure of consideration (*Steinberg v Scala (Leeds)* (1923)).	The Minors' Contracts Act 1987 now allows ratification on attaining the age of majority, and has given the courts wider powers to order the restoration of property acquired by a minor.

Minors' liability in tort

As there is no minimum age limit in relation to actions in tort, minors may be liable under a tortious action. The courts will not permit a party to enforce a contract indirectly by substituting an action in tort, or quasi-contract, for an action in contract (*Leslie v Shiell* (1914)).

Mental incapacity and intoxication

A contract by a person who is of unsound mind or under the influence of drink or drugs is *prima facie* valid.

To avoid a contract such a person must show:

- that their mind was so affected at the time that they were incapable of understanding the nature of their actions; and
- that the other party either knew or ought to have known of their disability.

In any case, they must pay a reasonable price for necessaries sold and delivered to them.

Privity

This refers to the rule that a contract can only impose rights or obligations on persons who are parties to it, so third parties cannot sue on the basis of a contract between two other parties (*Dunlop v Selfridge* (1915)).

There are, however, a number of consequences of the privity rule:

- the beneficiary sues in some other capacity: a third party can enforce a contract where they are legally appointed to administer the affairs of one of the original parties (*Beswick v Beswick* (1967));
- the situation involves a collateral contract: a collateral contract arises where one party promises something to

another party if that other party enters into a contract with a third party: eg, A promises to give B something if B enters into a contract with C. In such a situation the second party can enforce the original promise, ie, B can insist on A complying with the original promise (*Shanklin Pier v Detel Products Ltd* (1951));

⟳ there is a valid assignment of the benefit of the contract. a party to a contract can transfer the benefit of that contract to a third party through the formal process of assignment. The assignment must be in writing, and the assignee receives no better rights under the contract than the assignor possessed. The burden of a contract cannot be assigned without the consent of the other party to the contract;

⟳ it is foreseeable that damage caused will be passed on to a third party (*Linden Gardens Trust Ltd v Lenesta Sludge Disposals Ltd* (1994));

⟳ one of the parties has entered the contract as a trustee for a third party (*Les Affréteurs Réunis SA v Leopold Walford (London) Ltd* (1919));

⟳ the Contracts (Rights of Third Parties) Act 1999 allows third parties, named within the contract by class, name or description, to enforce contracts made for their benefit.

Intention to create legal relations

This principle operates to reduce the number of cases that courts have to deal with. The courts only have to deal with cases that the parties intended to make binding in the first place.

The test is an *objective* one, and the courts apply different *rebuttable presumptions* depending on the particular context of the case.

Domestic and social agreements	The presumption is that the parties do not intend to create legal relations (*Balfour v Balfour* (1919); *Simpkins v Pays* (1955); *Jones v Pandavatton* (1969)). Evidence can be brought to rebut the presumption (*Merritt v Merritt* (1970)).
Commercial agreements	The presumption is that the parties intend to create legal relations (*Edwards v Skyways* (1964)). It will usually take express wording to the contrary to avoid its operation (*Rose and Frank Co v Crompton Bros* (1925)). Agreements which are 'binding in honour' do not create legal relations (*Jones v Vernons Pools Ltd* (1938)).

Collective agreements

Agreements between employers and trade unions are commercial agreements, but are presumed not to give rise to legal relations (*Ford Motor Co v AUEFW* (1969)).

5 Contents of contracts

Forms of misrepresentation

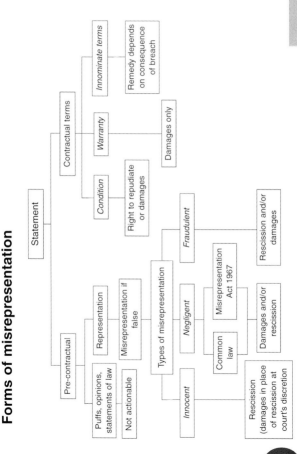

Not all statements made in negotiating contracts have the same legal effect. It is necessary to distinguish between contractual terms and mere representations.

Contractual terms	Part of contract. Remedy if false – breach of contract.
Tests	Where the statement is of such importance that the promisee would not have entered into the agreement without it (*Bannerman v White* (1861)). Where the statement is made by a party with special knowledge or skill (*Dick Bentley Productions Ltd v Harold Smith (Motors) Ltd* (1965)).
Mere representations	Not part of contract. Remedy if false – misrepresentation.
Tests	Where there is a time gap between the statement and the making of the contract (*Routledge v McKay* (1954)). Where the statement is oral, and the agreement is subsequently drawn up in written form (*Routledge v McKay* (1954)). Where the statement is made to a party with special knowledge or skill (*Oscar Chess Ltd v Williams* (1957)).

Conditions, warranties, and innominate terms

You must also distinguish between types of terms:

Conditions	A fundamental part of the agreement. Breach gives the right either to terminate the contract or to go through with the agreement and sue for damages (*Poussard v Spiers and Pond* (1876)).
Warranties	A subsidiary obligation in the agreement. Breach does not give the right to terminate the contract; only damages available (*Bettini v Gye* (1876)).
Innominate terms	The remedy depends on the consequence of the breach. If 'substantially the whole benefit of the contract' is lost, then repudiation is possible; if not, then only damages available (*Cehave v Bremer (The Hansa Nord)* (1976)).

Implied terms do not have to be stated, but are automatically introduced into the contract by implication. Implied terms can be divided into three types:

Terms implied by statute	For example, the Sale of Goods Act 1979 implies terms relating to description, satisfactory quality, and fitness for purpose into sale of goods contracts.
Terms implied by custom	An agreement may be subject to customary terms, not actually specified by the parties (*Hutton v Warren* (1836)). Custom cannot override the express terms of an agreement (*Les Affréteurs v Walford* (1919)).
Terms implied by the courts	On occasion, the court will presume that the parties intended to include a term which is not expressly stated. Done to give business efficacy to the contract (*The Moorcock* (1889)). Decided on the basis of 'the officious bystander' test.

Parol evidence rule

If all the terms of a contract are in writing, then there is a strong presumption that no evidence supporting a different oral agreement will be permitted to vary those terms (*Hutton v Watling* (1948)).

The presumption may be rebutted where the document was not intended to set out all the terms agreed on by the parties (*Re SS Ardennes* (1951)).

Exemption and exclusion clauses

An exemption clause is a term in a contract which tries to exempt, or limit, the liability of a party in breach of the agreement. They are controlled by a mixture of common law, the Unfair Contract Terms Act 1977 (UCTA), the Unfair Terms

Consumer Contracts Regulations 1994, and the various Acts which imply certain terms into particular contracts.

The following questions should always be asked with regard to exclusion clauses:

- Has the exclusion clause been incorporated into the contract?
- Does the exclusion clause effectively cover the breach?
- What effect do UCTA and the Unfair Terms in Consumer Contracts Regulations have on the exclusion clause?

Has the exclusion clause been incorporated into the contract?

An exclusion clause cannot be effective unless it is actually a term of a contract. There are three ways in which such a term may be inserted into a contractual agreement, as shown in the following chart.

Signature	If a person signs a contractual document, then they are bound by its terms, even if they did not read it (*L'Estrange v Graucob* (1934)). This rule may be avoided where the party seeking to rely on the exclusion clause misled the other party into signing the contract (*Curtis v Chemical Cleaning and Dyeing Co* (1951)).
Notice	In order for notice to be adequate, the document bearing the exclusion clause must be an integral part of the contract, and given at the time the contract is made (*Chapleton v Barry UDC* (1940) and *Olley v Marlborough Court Ltd* (1949)). The greater the exemption, the greater the degree of notice required (*Thornton v Shoe Lane Parking Ltd* (1971)).
Custom	Previous dealings on the basis of an exclusion clause may include the clause in later contracts (*Spurling v Bradshaw* (1956)). However, actual knowledge of the exclusion clause is required (*Hollier v Rambler Motors* (1972)).

Does the exclusion clause effectively cover the breach?

The *contra proferentem* rule requires any uncertainty or ambiguity in the exclusion clause to be interpreted against the meaning claimed for it by the person seeking to rely on it (*Andrews v Singer* (1934)).

What effect does the Unfair Contract Terms Act 1977 have on the exclusion clause?

Negligence	There is an absolute prohibition on exemption clauses in relation to liability in negligence resulting in death or injury (ss 2 and 5). Exemption clauses relating to liability for other damage caused by negligence will only be enforced to the extent that they satisfy the 'requirement of reasonableness' (s 2 and *Smith v Bush* (1989)).
Contract	These provisions apply in all consumer transactions, and non-consumer transactions where one party deals on the other's standard terms. Any exclusion clause which seeks to avoid liability for breach of contract is only valid to the extent that it complies with the 'requirement of reasonableness' (s 3). This test also applies where a clause seeks to permit a party to avoid performing the contract completely, or to permit performance less than reasonably expected.

The requirement of reasonableness means 'fair and reasonable ... having regard to the circumstances ...' (s 11).

Schedule 2 provides guidelines for the reasonableness test in regard to non-consumer transactions, but it is likely that similar considerations will be taken into account by the courts in consumer transactions. Amongst these considerations are:

○ the relative strength of the parties' bargaining power;
○ whether any inducement was offered in return for the limitation on liability;

- ⮕ whether the customer knew, or ought to have know about the existence or extent of the exclusion;
- ⮕ whether the goods were manufactured or adapted to th special order of the customer.

The application of the Act may be seen in *George Mitche (Chesterhall) Ltd v Finney Lock Seeds Ltd* (1983).

The Unfair Terms in Consumer Contracts Regulatior 1999, introduced to implement the European Unfair Contra Terms Directive, run in parallel with UCTA.

They apply to 'any term in a contract concluded betwee a seller or supplier and a consumer where the term has ne been individually negotiated' and are, therefore, wider scope than UCTA. They focus on the formal procedur through which contracts are made, rather than th substantive contents of the contract in question. They strik out terms which are unfair as being not entered into in goo faith. They also introduce a requirement that contracts shou be made in plain intelligible language and give the Directc General of Fair Trading and other qualifying bodies, eg th Consumers Association, the power to apply for injunctior against unfair terms.

6 Vitiating factors in contract

Mistake

Very few mistakes will affect the validity of a contract at common law, but where a mistake is operative, it will render the contract void. This has the effect that property transferred under operative mistake can be recovered, even where it has been transferred to an innocent third party.

It is usual to divide mistakes into the following three categories:

Common mistake	Both parties to an agreement share the same mistake. It must be of a fundamental nature. *Bell v Lever Bros Ltd* (1932) suggests that a mistake as to quality can never render an agreement void for mistake. *Res extincta* – the mistake is as to the existence of the subject matter of the contract (*Couturier v Hastie* (1856)).
Mutual mistake	The parties have different views of the situation, but they do not realise it. The court will try to decide which of the competing views of the situation a reasonable person would support, and the contract will be enforceable on such terms (*Smith v Hughes* (1871)).
Unilateral mistake	Only one of the parties to the agreement is mistaken and the other party is aware of it. Cases involving unilateral mistake mainly relate to identity. A contract will only be void for mistake where the seller intended to contract with a different person from the one with whom they actually did contract.

Common mistake	*Res sua* – the mistake is that one of the parties to the contract already owns what he is contracting to receive (*Cooper v Phibbs* (1867)). Equity may intervene in regard to common mistake, namely, setting an agreement aside completely or on particular terms (*Magee v Pennine Insurance Co Ltd* (1969)).
Mutual mistake	If the court is unable to decide the outcome on the basis of an objective 'reasonable person' test, then the contract will be void (*Raffles v Wichelhaus* (1864) and *Scriven Bros v Hindley and Co* (1913)).
Unilateral mistake	It is important to distinguish between misrepresentation and unilateral mistake – mistake makes a contract void, misrepresentation merely makes it voidable, and good title can be passed before the contract is avoided. This distinction will be seen in comparing *Ingram v Little* with *Phillips v Brooks*, and *Cundy v Lindsay* (1878) with *King's Norton Metal Co v Edridge, Merrit and Co* (1897).

Mistake in respect of documents

There are two mechanisms for dealing with mistakes in written contracts.

Rectification	An equitable doctrine which allows documents to be altered where they do not state the actual intentions of the parties (*Joscelyne v Nissen* (1970)).
Non est factum	Where someone signs a document under a misapprehension as to its true nature, the law may permit them to claim *non est factum*,ie, that the document is not their deed. The person signing the document must not have been careless (*Saunders v Anglia Building Society* (1970)).

Misrepresentation

Misrepresentation is a false statement of fact, made by one party before, or at the time of, the contract, which induces the other party to enter into the contract.

There must be a statement.

Silence does not generally amount to a representation, except:

⮕ where the statement is a half truth; it may be true, but misleading none the less (*Notts Patent Brick and Tile Co v Butler* (1886));

⮕ where the statement was true when made, but has subsequently become false before the contract is concluded (*With v O'Flanagan* (1936));

⮕ where the contract is *uberrimae fidei*, ie, made in utmost good faith; in such contracts there is a duty to disclose all material facts.

The following statements will not amount to a representation:

⮕ mere sales puffs (*Dimmock v Hallett* (1866));
⮕ statements of law;

- statements of opinion (*Bisset v Wilkinson* (1927)). If th person does not actually believe that the opinion the express is true, then an action for misrepresentation w be possible (*Edgington v Fitzmaurice* (1884)).

The statement must actually induce the contract:

- the statement must have been made by one party to th contract to the other, and not by a third party;
- the statement must have been addressed to the perso claiming to have been misled;
- the person claiming to have been misled must have bee aware of the statement;
- the person claiming to have been misled must hav relied on the statement (*Horsfall v Thomas* (1962)).

Types of misrepresentations

Misrepresentation can be divided into three types.

Fraudulent misrepresentation	Statement made, knowing it to be false, or believing it to be false, or recklessly careless whether it is true or false (*Derry v Peek* (1889)).
Negligent misrepresentation	Statement made in the belief that it is true, but without reasonable grounds for that belief.
Innocent misrepresentation	Statement made by a person who not only believes it to be true, but also has reasonable grounds for that belief.

Negligent misrepresentation can be divided further into two types.

At common law	The possibility of liability in negligence for misstatements arose from *Hedley Byrne and Co v Heller* (1964). In *Esso Petroleum v Mardon* (1976), Mardon succeeded in an action for negligent misstatement.
Misrepresentation Act 1967 (MA)	Reverses the common law burden of proof. Where a misrepresentation has been made, then under s 2(1) of the Act it is up to the party who made the statement to show that they had reasonable grounds for believing it to be true.

Remedies for misrepresentation

Fraudulent misrepresentation	Rescission, and/or damages.
Negligent misrepresentation	Rescission, and/or damages. Under the MA, the measure of damages still determined as in tort actions (*Royscot Trust Ltd v Rogerson* (1991)).
Innocent misrepresentation	Common law remedy is rescission. Under s 2(2) of the MA damages may be awarded instead of rescission.

With regard to s 2(2) of the MA, the court can usually only award damages where the remedy of rescission is still available (but see *Thomas Witter v TBP Industries* (1996)), and the right to rescind can be lost:

➲ by affirmation, either express or implied (*Leaf v International Galleries* (1950));

⮌ where the parties cannot be restored to their original positions;

⮌ where third parties have acquired rights in the subject matter of the contract (*Phillips v Brooks* (1919)).

Duress

If force, either physical or economic, is used to form a contract, then the contract is voidable at the instance of the innocent party (*Barton v Armstrong* (1975) and *North Ocean Shipping Co v Hyundai Construction* (1979)).

Claimants must show two things:

⮌ that pressure, which resulted in an absence of choice on their part, was brought to bear on them; and

⮌ that the pressure was of a nature considered illegitimate by the courts.

Undue influence

Transactions, either contract or gifts, may be avoided where they have been entered into as a consequence of the undue influence of the person benefiting from them. The effect of undue influence is to make a contract voidable, but delay may bar the right to avoid the agreement.

There are two possible situations relating to undue influence, shown in the following box.

Special relationship

There is a presumption that the transaction is the consequence of undue influence.

The burden of proof is on the person receiving the benefit to rebut the presumption (*Re Craig* (1971)).

Examples of special relationships are:

(a) parent and child while still a minor;
(b) guardian and ward;
(c) religious adviser and follower;
(d) doctor and patient;
(e) solicitor and client.

The list is not a closed one and other relationships may be included within the scope of the special relationship.

Even where a special relationship exists, a transaction will not be set aside unless it is shown to be disadvantageous (*National Westminster Bank v Morgan* (1985)), although *Barclays Bank plc v Coleman* (2003) (CA) questions whether the disadvantage needs to be 'manifest'.

No special relationship

The burden of proof is on the party claiming the protection of the undue influence doctrine.

The rule relating to manifest disadvantage, applying in relation to special relationships, does not apply where no special relationship exists (*CIBC Mortgages plc v Pitt* (1993)).

The key element in deciding whether a relationship was a special one or not was whether one party was in a position of dominance over the other (*National Westminster Bank v Morgan* (1985)).

Contracts in restraint of trade

A contract in restraint of trade is an agreement whereby one party restricts its future freedom to engage in their trade, business or profession. The general rule is that such agreements are *prima facie* void, but they may be valid if i can be shown that they meet the following requirements:

- the person imposing the restrictions has a legitimate interest to protect;
- the restriction is reasonable as between the parties; the restriction is not contrary to the public interest.

The doctrine of restraint of trade is flexible in its application and may be applied to new situations when they arise Bearing this in mind, however, it is usual to classify the branches of the doctrine as follows.

Restraints on employees	Employers cannot protect themselves against competition from an ex-employee, except where they have a legitimate interest to protect. The only legitimate interests recognised by the law are trade secrets, customer bases and stable workforce.
Restraints on vendors of business	Restrictions may legitimately be placed on previous owners to prevent them from competing, in the future, with new owners. The restraint should not be greater than is necessary to protect that interest (*British Concrete v Schelff* (1921)).
Restraints on distributors' solus agreements	This category of restraint of trade is usually concerned with solus agreements between petrol companies and garage proprietors.

Restraints on employees	Even in protecting those interests, the restraint must be of a reasonable nature. What constitutes 'reasonable' in this context depends on the circumstances of the case (*Lamson Pneumatic Tube Co v Phillips* (1904) and *Empire Meat Co Ltd v Patrick* (1939)). The longer the period of time covered by the restraint, the more likely it is to be struck down, but in *Fitch v Dewes* (1921), it was held that a lifelong restriction placed on a solicitor's clerk was valid.
Restraints on vendors of business	In *Nordenfeld v Maxim Nordenfeld Guns and Ammunition Co* (1894), a worldwide restraint on competition was held to be enforceable.
Restraints on distributors' solus agreements	Petrol companies have a legitimate interest to protect, and the outcome depends on whether the restraint obtained in protection of that interest is reasonable (*Esso Petroleum v Harper's* (1968)). *Esso v Harper's* does not create a rule that any solus agreement involving a restriction which was to last longer than five years must be void as being in restraint of trade. Each case depends on its particular circumstances (*Alec Lobb (Garages) Ltd v Total Oil Ltd* (1985)).

Exclusive service contracts are structured to exploit one of the parties, by controlling and limiting their output, rather than assisting them. The most famous cases involve musicians (eg *Schroeder Music Publishing Co v Macauley* (1974)).

7 Discharge of contracts

Discharge of contract means that the parties to an agreement are freed from their contractual obligations.

A contract is discharged in one of four ways:

- agreement;
- performance;
- frustration;
- breach.

Discharge by agreement

The contract itself may contain provision for its discharge, by either the passage of a fixed period of time, or the happening of a particular event.

Alternatively, it may provide, either expressly or by implication, that one or other of the parties can bring it to an end, as in a contract of employment.

Where there is no such provision in a contract, another contract is required to cancel it before all the obligations have been met. There are two possible situations.

Where the contract is executory	The mutual exchange of promises to release one another from future performance will be sufficient consideration.
Where the contract is executed	The other party must provide consideration to be released from their part of the contract; this is accord and satisfaction.

Discharge by performance

This is the normal way in which contracts are discharged. As a general rule, discharge requires complete and exact performance of the obligations in the contract (*Cutter v Power* (1795)).

There are four exceptions to the general rule requiring complete performance:

- where the contract is divisible (*Bolton v Mahadeva* (1972));
- where the contract is capable of being fulfilled by substantial performance (*Hoenig v Isaacs* (1952));
- where performance has been prevented by the other party;
- where partial performance has been accepted by the other party.

Discharge by frustration

The doctrine of frustration permits a party to a contract, in the following circumstances, to be excused performance on the grounds of impossibility, arising after the formation of the contract:

- destruction of the subject matter of the contract has occurred (*Taylor v Caldwell* (1863));
- government interference, or supervening illegality, prevents performance (*Re Shipton and Co* (1915));
- a particular event, which is the sole reason for the contract, fails to take place (*Krell v Henry* (1903)); this only applies where the cancelled event was the sole purpose of the contract (*Herne Bay Steamboat Co v Hutton* (1903));

⤵ the commercial purpose of the contract is defeated (*Jackson v Union Marine Insurance Co* (1874));
⤵ in the case of a contract of personal service, the party dies or becomes otherwise incapacitated (*Condor v Barron Knights* (1966)).

Frustration will not apply where:

⤵ the parties have made express provision in the contract for the event which has occurred;
⤵ the frustrating event is self-induced (*Maritime National Fish Ltd v Ocean Trawlers Ltd* (1935));
⤵ an alternative method of performance is still possible (*Tsakiroglou and Co v Noblee and Thorl* (1962));
⤵ the contract simply becomes more expensive to perform (*Davis Contractors v Fareham UDC* (1956)).

The effect of frustration

At common law, the effect of frustration was to make the contract void as from the time of the frustrating event.

⤵ money paid is recoverable;
⤵ money due to be paid ceases to be payable;
⤵ the parties may be permitted to retain expenses incurred from any money received, or recover those expenses from money due to be paid before the frustrating event;
⤵ where a party has gained a valuable benefit under the contract he may be required to pay a reasonable sum in respect of it.

Discharge by breach

Breach of a contract occurs where one of the parties to the agreement fails to comply, either completely or satisfactorily, with their obligations under it.

A breach of contract may occur in three ways:

- where a party, prior to the time of performance, states that they will not fulfil their contractual obligation;
- where a party fails to perform their contractual obligation;
- where a party performs their obligation in a defective manner.

Anticipatory breach

This is where one party, prior to the actual due date of performance, demonstrates an intention not to perform their obligations. The intention not to fulfil the contract can be either express (*Hochster v De La Tour* (1853)) or implied (*Omnium D'Enterprises v Sutherland* (1919)).

The innocent party can sue for damages immediately, as in *Hochster v De La Tour*, or can wait until the time for performance before taking action. In the latter instance, they are entitled to make preparations for performance, and claim the agreed contract price (*White and Carter (Councils) v McGregor* (1961)).

Remedies for breach of contract

The principal remedies for breach of contract are:

- damages;
- *quantum meruit*;
- specific performance;
- injunction.

Damages

The estimation of what damages are to be paid by a party in breach of contract can be divided into two parts: remoteness and measure of damages.

Remoteness of damage	The rule in *Hadley v Baxendale* (1845) states that damages will only be awarded in respect of losses which either arise naturally, *or* which both parties may reasonably be supposed to have contemplated, when the contract was made, as a probable result of its breach. The party in breach can only be held liable for abnormal consequences where they have actual knowledge that the abnormal consequences might follow (*Victoria Laundry Ltd v Newham Industries Ltd* (1949) and *The Heron II* (*Czarnikow v Koufos*) (1967)).
Measure of damages	The aim is to put the injured party in the same position he would have been in had the contract been properly performed. The market rule: the buyer is entitled to buy similar goods, and pay the market price prevailing at the time. They can then claim the difference in price between what they paid and the original contract price as damages, and conversely if a buyer refuses to accept goods. The duty to mitigate losses: the buyer of goods which are not delivered has to buy the replacements as cheaply as possible; and the seller of goods has to try to get as good a price as he can when he sells them (*Payzu v Saunders* (1919)).

Non-pecuniary loss can be recovered (*Jarvis v Swan Tours Ltd* (1973)).

Liquidated damages and penalties

Liquidated damages	Are a genuine pre-estimate of loss for breach of contract. The court will recognise and apply such estimates.
Penalties	Are to punish the person in breach rather than to compensate the other party. If the court considers the provision to be a penalty, it will not give it effect, but will award damages in the normal way (*Dunlop v New Garage and Motor Co* (1915)).

Quantum meruit

This means that a party should be awarded 'as much as they have earned'.

If the parties enter into a contractual agreement without determining the reward that is to be provided for performance, then in the event of any dispute, the court will award a reasonable sum.

Payment may also be claimed on the basis of *quantum meruit* where a party has carried out work in respect of a void contract (*Craven-Ellis v Canons Ltd* (1936)).

Specific performance

It will sometimes suit a party to break their contractual obligations, and pay damages; but, through an order for specific performance, the party in breach may be instructed to complete their part of the contract:

- an order of specific performance will only be granted in cases where the common law remedy of damages is inadequate;

specific performance will not be granted where the court cannot supervise its enforcement (*Ryan v Mutual Tontine Westminster Chambers Association* (1893)).

Injunction

This is also an equitable order of the court, which directs a person not to break their contract. It can have the effect of indirectly enforcing contracts for personal service (*Warner Bros v Nelson* (1937)).

An injunction will only be granted to enforce negative covenants within the agreement, and cannot be used to enforce positive obligations (*Whitwood Chemical Co v Hardman* (1891)).

8 Agency

Definition

An agent is a person who is empowered to represent another legal party, called the principal, and brings the principal into a legal relationship with a third party.

Agency agreements may be either contractual or gratuitous.

Types of agency

There are four types of agent:

- a general agent has the power to act for a principal generally in relation to a particular area of business;
- a special agent only has the authority to act in one particular transaction;
- a *del credere* agent, for an additional commission, guarantees payment to the principal;
- a commission agent owes the duties of an agent to his principal but contracts with the third party as a principal in his own right.

Creation of agency

Agency requires the consent of the principal (*White v Lucas* (1887)), but consent may be implied.

Agency may be created expressly or may arise in the following ways:

Ratification Where a person who has no authority purports to contract with a third party on behalf of a principal, the principal may elect to adopt the contract and give retrospective validity to the action of the purported agent.

The principal must have been in existence at the time the agent entered into the contract (*Kelner v Baxter* (1866)).

The principal must have had legal capacity to enter into the contract when it was made.

Implication Arises from the relationship that exists between the principal and the agent.

It is assumed that the principal has given authority to the other person to act as his agent. Authority to act as agent is implied from the particular position held by the individual (*Panorama Developments v Fidelis Furnishing Fabrics Ltd* (1971)).

Problems most often occur in relation to the implied extent of a person's authority and can arise in relation to appointment (*Hely-Hutchinson v Brayhead Ltd* (1967)).

Necessity Occurs under circumstances where, although there is no agreement between the parties, an emergency requires that an agent take particular action in order to protect the interests of the principal.

There must be a genuine emergency (*Great Northern Railway Co v Swaffield* (1874)).

There must also be no practical way of obtaining further instructions from the principal (*Springer v Great Western Railway Co* (1921)).

Estoppel

Holding out can make a person liable for the actions of a purported agent, although it does not actually create an agency relationship. It arises where the principal has led other parties to believe that a person has the authority to represent him. Then, even although no principal-agency relationship actually exists in fact, the principal is prevented (estopped) from denying the existence of the agency relationship and is bound by the action of his purported agent as regards any third party who acted in the belief of its existence.

To rely on agency by estoppel, the principal must have made a representation as to the authority of the agent (*Freeman and Lockyer v Buckhurst Park Properties Ltd* (1964)).

As with estoppel generally, the party seeking to use it must have relied on the representation (*Overbrooke Estates Ltd v Glencombe Properties Ltd* (1974)).

Nature of agent's authority

Actual authority This can arise in one of two ways:

(a) express actual authority is explicitly granted by the principal to the agent;

(b) implied actual authority increases the scope of express authority. Third parties are entitled to assume that agents holding a particular position have all the powers that are usually provided to such an agent (*Watteau v Fenwick* (1893)).

Apparent authority This can also arise in two ways:

(a) where a representation is made that a person has the authority to act as agent without actually appointing the agent – see agency by estoppel (*Freeman and Lockyer v Buckhurst Park Properties Ltd* (1964));

(b) where a principal revokes an agent's authority without informing third parties who had previously dealt with the agent (*Willis Faber and Co Ltd v Joyce* (1911)).

Warrant of authority

If an agent contracts with a third party on behalf of a principal, the agent impliedly guarantees that the principal exists and has contractual capacity, and that he has that person's authority to act as his agent. If such is not the case, the agent is personally liable to third parties for breach of warrant of authority (*Yonge v Toynbee* (1910)).

Duties and rights of agents

Duties of an agent	To perform the undertaking according to instructions (*Turpin v Bilton* (1843)). To exercise due care and skill (*Keppel v Wheeler* (1927)). To carry out instructions personally. To account. Not to permit a conflict of interest to arise (*McPherson v Watt* (1877)). Not to make a secret profit or misuse confidential information (*Boardman v Phipps* (1967)). Not to take a bribe (*Mahesan v Malaysian Government Officers Co-operative Housing Society* (1978)).
Rights of an agent	To claim remuneration for services performed. In commercial agreements, the courts will imply a term requiring the payment of a reasonable remuneration. To claim indemnity for all expenses legitimately incurred in the performance of services. To exercise a lien over property owned by the principal.

Where the principal's existence is not disclosed:

- the agent can enforce the contract against the third party;
- the principal can enforce the contract against the third party;
- the third party can choose to enforce the contract against the agent or the principal;
- the undisclosed principal cannot ratify any contract made outside of the agent's actual authority;

- the principal may be excluded from the contract if the third party had a special reason to contract with the agent (*Greer v Downs Supply Co* (1927));
- the third party may not be bound by the contract if the agent misrepresents the identity of the principal (*Archer Stone* (1898)).

Payment by means of an agent

If the agent does not pay the third party, the principal remains liable.

If the agent absconds with money paid by the third party then, if the principal is undisclosed, he sustains the loss; if however, the principal is disclosed, the agent must have had authority to accept money or else the third party is liable.

Termination of agency

Agreements usually may end:

- by mutual agreement;
- by the unilateral action of one of the parties;
- through frustration;
- due to the death, insanity or bankruptcy of either of the parties.

9 Partnership law

Definition of partnership

Section 1 of the Partnership Act (PA)1890 states that partnership is the relation which subsists between persons carrying on a business in common with a view to profit'.

Simply receiving a payment from profits is not sufficient automatically to make a person a partner in a business concern.

Legal status of a partnership

A partnership has no separate legal personality apart from its members in the way a joint-stock company does.

Partnerships are generally limited to 20 members; however, certain professional partnerships are exempt from this maximum limit.

Formation of a partnership

There are no specific legal requirements governing the formation of a partnership. Partnerships arise from the agreement of the parties involved and are governed by the general principles of contract law. The PA tends to serve as a default where the partners do not provide for their own operation.

The partnership agreement is an internal document and does not necessarily affect the rights of third parties.

Duties of partners

The legal nature of the partnership involves a complicated mixture of elements of contract, agency and equity:

- the partnership agreement is contractual;
- partners are, at one and the same time, both agents of the firm and their fellow partners, and principals as regards those other partners;
- partners are in a fiduciary position in relation to one another and subject to the equitable rights and duties that derive from that relationship.

Sections 28–30 of the PA lay down specific duties as follows

- the duty of disclosure (s 28; *Law v Law* (1905));
- the duty to account (s 29; *Bentley v Craven* (1953));
- the duty not to compete (s 30).

Rights of partners

Subject to express provision to the contrary in the partnership agreement, s 24 of the PA sets out the rights of partners. Amongst the most important of these are the rights:

- to share equally in the capital and profits of the business;
- to be indemnified by the firm for any liabilities incurred or payments made in the course of the firm's business;
- to take part in the management of the business;
- to have access to the firm's books;
- to prevent the admission of a new partner;
- to prevent any change in the nature of the partnership business.

Partnership property

It is important to distinguish between partnership property and personal property for the following reasons:

- partnership property must be used exclusively for partnership purposes;

- any increase in the value of partnership property belongs to the partnership;
- any increase in the value of personal property belongs to the person who owns the property;
- on the dissolution of the firm, partnership property is used to pay debts before personal property;
- partnership and personal property are treated differently in the satisfaction of claims made by partnership creditors as opposed to personal creditors;
- on the death of a partner, any interest in partnership land will pass as personalty, whereas land owned personally will pass as realty.

The authority of partners to bind the firm

Each partner has the power to bind co-partners and make them liable on business transactions.

Authority can be actual or implied on the basis of the usual authority possessed by a partner in the particular line of business carried out by the firm (*Mercantile Credit v Garrod* (1962)).

Every partner, other than a limited partner, is presumed to have the implied authority to enter into the following transactions:

- to sell the firm's goods;
- to buy goods of a kind normally required by the firm;
- to engage employees;
- to employ a solicitor to act for the firm in defence of an action or in pursuit of a debt.

Partners in trading have the following additional implied powers:

- to accept, draw, issue, or indorse bills of exchange c other negotiable instruments on behalf of the firm;
- to borrow money on the credit of the firm;
- to pledge the firm's goods as security for borrowe money.

Partners' liability on debts

Every partner is responsible for the full amount of the firm' liability: there is no limited liability in ordinary partnerships Outsiders have the choice of taking action against the firr collectively, or against the individual partners. Wher damages are recovered from one partner only, the othe partners are under a duty to contribute equally to the amour paid.

Partners may liable for debts, contracts and for torts.

The Limited Partnership Act 1907 allows for the formatio of limited partnerships, subject to the following rules:

- limited partners are not liable for partnership deb beyond the extent of their capital contribution, but in th ordinary course of events they are not permitted t remove their capital;
- one or more of the partners must retain full, ie, unlimited liability for the debts of the partnership;
- a partner with limited liability is not permitted to take pa in the management of the business enterprise an cannot usually bind the partnership in any transactior Contravention of this rule will result in the loss of limite liability;
- the partnership must be registered with the Companie Registry.

10 Company law

Corporations and their legal characteristics

Types of corporations

Companies differ from partnerships in that they are bodies corporate.

Corporations can be created in one of three ways.

By grant of royal charter	These are governed mainly by the common law. They tend to be restricted to professional, educational and charitable institutions and are not used in relation to business enterprises.
By special Act of Parliament	Known as statutory corporations. Although common during the 19th century, particularly in relation to railway and public utility companies, they are not greatly used nowadays, and certainly not by ordinary trading companies.
By registration under the Companies Acts	Since 1844, companies have acquired the status of a corporation simply by complying with the requirements for registration set out in general Acts of Parliament. This is the method by which the great majority of trading enterprises are incorporated.

The doctrine of separate personality

Separate personality: the company exists as a legal person in its own right, completely distinct from the members who own shares in it (*Salomon v Salomon and Co* (1887)).

Consequences of separate personality

Limited liability

This refers to the fact that the potential liability shareholders is fixed at a maximum level equal to the nomin value of the shares held.

Perpetual succession

This refers to the fact the company continues to exi irrespective of any change in its membership. The compar ceases to exist only when it is formally wound up.

The company owns the business property in its own righ shareholders do not own the assets of a business, they ow shares in that business (*Macaura v Northern Assuranc* (1925)).

The company has *contractual capacity* in its own right an can sue and be sued in its own name: members, as such, ar not able to bind the company.

The rule in *Foss v Harbottle*

Where a company suffers an injury, it is for the company acting through the majority of the members, to take th appropriate remedial action; an individual cannot raise a action in response to a wrong suffered by the company.

Lifting the veil of incorporation

There are a number of occasions when the doctrine c separate personality will not be followed.

Under the companies legislation	Section 24 of the Companies Act 1985 (CA) provides for personal liability of the member where a company carries on trading with fewer than two members. Section 229 requires consolidated accounts to be prepared by a group of related companies. Section 213 of the Insolvency Act 1986 provides for personal liability in relation to fraudulent trading. Section 214 does the same in relation to wrongful trading.
At common law	The courts will not permit the corporate form to be used for a clearly fraudulent purpose or to evade a legal duty (*Gilford Motor Co Ltd v Horne* (1933)). The courts are prepared to ignore separate personality in times of war where shareholders are enemy aliens (*Daimler Co Ltd v Continental Tyre and Rubber Co (GB) Ltd* (1917)). In groups of companies the courts will usually not ignore the separate existence of the various companies unless they are being used for fraud (*DHN Food Distributors Ltd v Borough of Tower Hamlets* (1976); but also *Woolfson v Strathclyde RC* (1978); and *National Dock Labour Board v Pinn and Wheeler* (1989)).

Types of companies

Although the distinction between public and private companies is probably the most important, there are number of ways in which companies can be classified, as follows.

Unlimited companies	Companies can be formed without limited liability. They get all the benefits of incorporation except limited liability.
Limited companies	The maximum liability of shareholders is fixed and cannot be increased without their agreement.

Limited and unlimited companies

Limited liability may be created in two ways.

By shares	Liability is limited to the amount remaining unpaid on shares held. If the full nominal value of the shares is paid, then shareholders have no further responsibility for company debts.
By guarantee	Usually restricted to non-trading enterprises, such as charities and professional and educational bodies. Liability is limited to an agreed amount which is only called on if the company cannot pay its debts on being wound up.

Public and private companies

Private companies	Tend to be small scale enterprises owned and operated by a small number of individuals. They cannot offer their shares to the public at large. Their shares are not quoted on any share market and tend not to be freely transferable.
Public limited companies	Tend to be large, and are usually controlled by directors and managers rather than owners. They are sources of investment and have freely transferable shares which are quoted on the Stock Exchange.

Legal differences between public and private companies

Public and private companies differ in that:

- public companies must have at least two directors, whereas private companies need only have one;
- public companies have minimum-issued and paid-up capital;
- the requirement to keep accounting records is shorter for private companies;
- the controls over distribution of dividend payments are relaxed in relation to private companies;
- private companies may purchase their own shares out of capital, but public companies cannot;
- private companies can provide financial assistance for the purchase of their own shares, but public companies cannot;
- there are fewer and looser controls over directors in private companies, as regards their financial relationships with their companies;

- private companies can make use of written resolutions
  private companies may also pass elective resolutions.

Registration

A registered company is incorporated when particula
documents are delivered to the registrar of companies (s 10)

On registration of these documents the registrar issues a
certificate of incorporation (s 13).

A private company may start its business as soon as the
certificate of registration is issued. A public company
however, cannot start business until it has obtained an
additional certificate from the registrar under s 117.

Documents required under s 10 are:

- a memorandum of association;
- articles of association (unless Table A articles are to
  apply);
- a statement detailing the first directors and secretary of
  the company, with their written consent and the address
  of the company's registered office;
- a statutory declaration that the necessary requirements
  of the CA have been complied with.

The constitution of the company

The constitution of a company is established by two
documents: the memorandum of association and the articles
of association. If there is any conflict between them, the
contents of the memorandum prevail over anything to the
contrary contained in the articles.

The memorandum of association

This governs the company's external affairs and must contain the following clauses:

(a) *name clause*: private companies are required to end their names either with the word 'Limited' or the abbreviation 'Ltd'; and public companies must end their names with the words 'public limited company' or the abbreviation 'plc';

(b) *registered office clause*: this states the company's legal address;

(c) *objects clause*: companies can now register as 'a general commercial company' which will empower them to 'carry on any trade or business whatsoever' (s 3A);

(d) *limited liability clause*: states that the liability of the members is limited;

(e) *authorised share capital clause*: states the maximum amount of share capital that a company is authorised to issue.

Association clause: states that the subscribers to the memorandum wish to form a company.

Public companies must have a clause stating that they are public companies.

The articles of association

These regulate the internal workings of the company. They form a contract between:

(a) the company and the company;

(b) the members and the company;

(c) the members.

They deal with such matters as the allotment and transfer of shares, the rights attaching to particular shares, the rules relating to the holding of meetings, and the powers of directors.

Companies can draw up their own articles or use Table A model articles. If articles are not submitted then Table A applies automatically.

Articles can be altered by the passing of a special resolution as long as it is done '*bona fide in the interest of the company as a whole*' (*Greenhalgh v Arderne Cinemas Ltd* (1951); *Brown v British Abrasive Wheel Co* (1919); *Sidebottom v Kershaw Leese and Co* (1920)).

Capital

The money companies need to finance their operation may be raised in the form of share capital or loan capital.

Share capital

A share has been defined as 'the interest of the shareholder in the company measured by a sum of money, for the purposes of liability in the first place and of interest in the second, but also consisting of a series of mutual covenants entered into by all the shareholders' (*Borland's Trustees v Steel* (1901)).

Types of shares

Shares can be divided into ordinary, preference, and redeemable shares.

Ordinary shares	These carry the greatest risk, but in recompense receive the greatest return.
Preference shares	These may have priority over ordinary shares in respect to dividends and re-payment. They carry a fixed rate of dividend.
Redeemable shares	These are issued on the basis that they may be bought back later by the company. Companies can now purchase their own shares, and are no longer restricted to buying redeemable shares.

Loan capital

The term *debenture* refers to the document which acknowledges the fact that a company has borrowed money, and also refers to the actual debt.

Debentures differ from shares in the following respects:

- debenture holders are creditors of the company; they are not members as shareholders are
- as creditors, debenture holders receive interest on their loans; they do not receive dividends as shareholders do;
- debenture holders are entitled to receive interest whether the company is profitable or not, even if the payment is made out of the company's capital;
- debenture may be issued at a discount.

Company charges

Debentures usually provide security for the amount loaned. There are two types of security for company loans, as shown below.

Fixed charge	A specific asset of the company is made subject to a charge in order to secure a debt. The company cannot thereafter dispose of the property without permission. If the company fails to honour its commitments, then the debenture holders can sell the asset to recover the money owed.
Floating charge	A floating charge does not attach to any specific property of the company until it crystallises. The security is provided by all the property owned by the company, some of which may be continuously changing. It permits the company to deal with its property without the need to seek permission.

Registration of charges

All charges have to be registered with the Companies Registry within 21 days of their creation. If not registered, then a charge is void against any other creditor, or the liquidator of the company, but it is still valid against the company.

In addition, companies are required to maintain a register of all charges on their property.

Priority of charges

Charges of the same type take priority according to their date of creation. As regards charges of different types, a fixed charge takes priority over a floating charge, even if it was created after the floating charge.

Directors

The board of directors is the agent of the company and may exercise all the powers of the company. Individual directors may be described as being in a *fiduciary relationship* with their companies.

Appointment of directors

The first directors are usually named in the articles or memorandum. Subsequent directors are appointed under the procedure stated in the articles. The usual procedure is for the company to elect the directors by an ordinary resolution in general meeting.

Casual vacancies are usually filled by the board of directors co-opting someone to act as director. That person then serves until the next *annual general meeting*, when they must stand for election in the usual manner.

Removal of directors

There are a number of ways in which a person may be obliged to give up his position as a director, as shown below.

Rotation	Table A provides that one-third of the directors shall retire at each AGM, being those with longest service. They are, however, open to re-election.
Retirement	Directors of public companies are required to retire at the first AGM after their 70th birthday.
Removal	A director can be removed at any time by the passing of an ordinary resolution of the company (s 303 of the CA). The company must be given special notice (28 days) of the intention to propose such a resolution. The power to remove a director under s 303 cannot be removed, but it can be avoided in private companies by the use of weighted voting rights (*Bushell v Faith* (1969)).

Disqualification

The articles of association usually provide for the disqualification of directors on grounds of: bankruptcy, mental illness, or prolonged absence from board meetings.

In addition, individuals can be disqualified from acting as directors for up to a maximum period of 15 years under the Company Directors Disqualification Act 1986.

Grounds for disqualification include:

- persistent breach of the companies legislation;
- committing offence in relation to companies;
- fraudulent trading;
- general unfitness.

Power of directors as a board

Article 70 of Table A provides that the directors of a company may exercise all the powers of the company. This power is given to the board as a whole and not to individual directors, although Art 72 does allow for the delegation of the board's powers to one or more directors.

The power of individual directors

There are three ways in which the power of the board of directors may be extended to individual directors.

Express actual authority	This arises from the express conferral by the board of a particular authority onto an individual director. For example, it is possible for the board to authorise an individual director specifically to negotiate and bind the company to a particular transaction.
Implied actual authority	This flows from the person's position. Appointment as managing director will give that person the *implied authority* to bind the company in the same way as the board, whose delegate they are (*Hely-Hutchinson v Brayhead Ltd* (1968)).
Apparent authority	Where a director is held out by the other members of the board as having the authority to bind the company, if a third party acts on such a representation, the company will be estopped from denying its truth (*Freeman and Lockyer v Buckhurst Park Properties (Mangal) Ltd* (1964)).

Directors' duties

As fiduciaries, directors owe the following duties to their company:

- the duty to act *bona fide* in the interests of the company: directors are under an obligation to act in what they genuinely believe to be the interest of the company;

- the duty not to act for any collateral purpose: directors cannot be said to acting *bona fide* if they use their powers for some ulterior or collateral purpose (*Howard Smith v Ampol Petroleum* (1974); and *Hogg v Cramphorn* (1967)). The breach of such a fiduciary duty is capable of ratification (*Bamford v Bamford* (1970));

- the duty not to permit a conflict of interest and duty to arise: this rule is strictly applied by the courts (*Regal (Hastings) v Gulliver* (1942)).

Duty of care and skill

Common law did not place any great burden on directors in this regard. *Re City Equitable Fire Assurance Co* (1925) established three points:

- a subjective test meant that a director was expected to show the degree of skill which might be reasonably expected of a person of their knowledge and experience;

- the duties of directors were held to be of an intermittent nature and they were not required to give continuous attention to the affairs of their company;

- in the absence of any grounds for suspicion, directors were entitled to leave the day to day operation of the company's business in the hands of managers.

Statute introduced wrongful trading by s 214 of the Insolvency Act 1986. Section 214 applies where a company is being wound up and it appears that at some time before the start of the winding up, a director knew, or ought to have known, that there was no reasonable chance of the company avoiding insolvent liquidation. In such circumstances, then, unless directors took every reasonable step to minimise the potential loss to the company's creditors, they may be liable to contribute such money to the assets of the company as the court thinks proper (*Re Produce Marketing Consortium Ltd* (1989)).

Company secretary

Section 744 of the CA includes the company secretary amongst the officers of a company. Every company must have a company secretary and although there are no specific qualifications required to perform such a role in a private company, s 286 of the CA requires that the directors of public company must ensure that the company secretary has the requisite knowledge and experience to discharge their functions. Section 286(2) sets out a list of professional bodies, membership of which enables a person to act as a company secretary.

Although old authorities, such as *Houghton and Co v Northard Lowe and Wills* (1928) suggest that company secretaries have extremely limited authority to bind their company, later cases have recognised the reality of the contemporary situation, whereby company secretaries potentially have extensive powers to bind their companies (*Panorama Developments Ltd v Fidelis Furnishing Fabrics Ltd* (1971)).

Company meetings

There are three types of meeting.

Annual general meeting	Every company is required to hold an annual general meeting (AGM) every calendar year, subject to a maximum period of 15 months. Private companies, subject to approval by a unanimous vote, may dispense with the holding of annual general meetings.
Extraordinary general meeting	An extraordinary general meeting (EGM) is any meeting other than an AGM. EGMs are usually called by the directors, although members holding 10% of the voting shares may requisition such a meeting.
Class meeting	This refers to the meeting of a particular class of shareholder, ie, those who hold a type of share providing particular rights, such as preference shares.

Types of resolutions

There are essentially three types of resolution.

Ordinary resolution	This requires a simple majority of those voting. Members who do not attend, or who attend but do not vote, are disregarded. Notice in relation to an ordinary resolution depends on the type of meeting at which it is proposed, 21 days for an AGM and 14 days for an EGM. In relation to an ordinary resolution to remove a director, the company must be given special notice of 28 days.
Extraordinary resolution	This requires a majority of not less than three quarters of those voting. An extraordinary resolution requires a minimum of 14 days' notice, but if it is to be voted on at an AGM, notice of 21 days will be required.
Special resolution	This also requires a majority of not less than three quarters, but in all circumstances, members must be given 21 days' notice of its contents.

Private companies can pass *elective resolutions* to dispense with particular formalities such as laying accounts before the AGM or, indeed, holding the AGM. They require the unanimous approval of the members.

Majority rule and minority protection

The majority usually dictate the action of a company and the minority is usually bound by the decisions of the majority (*Foss v Harbottle* (1843)). Problems arise where those in effective control of a company use their power to benefit themselves or cause a detriment to the minority shareholders.

Problems may arise where those in effective control of a company use their power in such a way as either to benefit themselves or to cause a detriment to the minority shareholders. In the light of such a possibility, the law has intervened to offer protection to minority shareholders. The source of the protection may be considered in three areas:

- *fraud on the minority*: it has long established at common law that those controlling the majority of shares are not to be allowed to use their position of control to perpetrate what is known as a fraud on the minority. In such circumstances, the individual shareholder will be able to take legal action in order to remedy their situation (*Cook v Deeks* (1916));

- *just and equitable winding up*: s 122(g) of the Insolvency Act 1986 gives the court the power to wind up a company if it considers it just and equitable to do so (*Re Yenidje Tobacco Co Ltd* (1916));

- *unfairly prejudicial conduct*: under s 459 of the CA, any member may petition the court for an order on the grounds that the affairs of the company are being conducted in a way that is unfairly prejudicial to the interests of some of the members. Section 461 gives the court general discretion as to any order it makes to remedy the situation (*Re London School of Electronics* (1986); *Re Bird Precision Bellows Ltd* (1984); *Re Sam Weller and Sons Ltd* (1990)).

In addition to the above remedies, the Secretary of State has the power under s 431 of the CA to appoint inspectors to investigate the affairs of a company.

Winding up and administration

Liquidation is the process whereby the life of the legal person the company is brought to an end.

There are three possible procedures:

- compulsory winding up;
- members' voluntary winding up;
- creditors' voluntary winding up.

Administration

This is a relatively new procedure, aimed at saving the business as a going concern by taking control of the company out of the hands of its directors and placing it in the hands of an of an administrator. Alternatively, the procedure is aimed at maximising the realised value of the business assets.

Once an administration order has been issued, it is no longer possible to commence winding up proceedings against the company or enforce charges, retention of title clauses or even hire purchase agreements against the company.

Insider dealing

This is governed by Pt V of the Criminal Justice Act (CJA)1993 which repeals and replaces the Company Securities (Insider Dealings) Act 1985.

Section 52 of the CJA states that an individual who has information as an insider is guilty of insider dealing if he deals in securities that are price affected in relation to the information. He is also guilty of an offence if he encourages others to deal in securities that are linked with this information.

Section 56 makes it clear that securities are 'price affected' in relation to inside information if the information would, if made public, be likely to have a significant effect on the price of those securities.

Section 57 defines an insider as a person who knows that he has inside information and knows that he has the information from an inside source. This section also states that 'inside source' refers to information acquired through being a director, employee or shareholder of an issuer of securities, or having access to information by virtue of their employment. Additionally, and importantly, it also treats as insiders those who acquire their information from those primary insiders previously mentioned.

There are a number of defences to a charge of insider dealing. For example, s 53 makes it clear that no person can be so charged if he did not expect the dealing to result in any profit or the avoidance of any loss.

On summary conviction, an individual found guilty of insider dealing is liable to a fine not exceeding the statutory maximum and/or a maximum of six months' imprisonment. On indictment, the penalty is an unlimited fine and/or a maximum of seven years' imprisonment.

11 Negligence

If a person injures another or damages property as a result of his negligent actions, he may be liable to pay compensation for this damage. However, to be liable in negligence the claimant must show on a balance of probabilities the following:

- duty of care;
- breach of duty;
- resultant damage.

Duty of care

The defendant must take reasonable care to avoid acts and omissions which could reasonably be foreseen to injure his or her neighbour. A neighbour is defined as someone so closely and directly affected by the act of the defendant that they would reasonably have been in contemplation as being so affected (*Donoghue v Stevenson* (1932)).

A three stage test was expounded in *Caparo Industries plc v Dickman* (1990):

- Was the harm caused reasonably foreseeable?
- Was there a relationship of proximity between the defendant and the claimant?
- In all the circumstances, is it just, fair and reasonable to impose attentive care?

This approach was supported in *Marc Rich v Bishop Rock Marine* (1995).

Policy reasons therefore may acceptably limit the existence of the duty of care (*Hill v Chief Constable of West Yorkshire* (1990)).

Nervous shock

Where the claimant claims damages for nervous shock, the question of proximity between the claimant and defendant may be critical to the success of that claim. Nervous shock or post-traumatic stress disorder must take the form of a recognised mental illness and this type of injury must be reasonably foreseeable:

- ⮑ passers-by may be expected to have the 'necessary phlegm and fortitude' not to suffer nervous shock as a result of seeing the aftermath of an accident (*Bourhill v Young* (1943));
- ⮑ fear for one's own safety may provide grounds for a claim (*Dulieu v White* (1991));
- ⮑ fear for the safety of a close relative may also be acceptable (*Hambrook v Stokes Bros* (1925); *McLoughlin v O'Brian* (1982)).

The definitive test is to be found in *Alcock and Others v Chief Constable of South Yorkshire* (1991), which established that there must be:

- ⮑ a close and loving relationship with the victim;
- ⮑ proximity in time and place to the accident or its aftermath;
- ⮑ nervous shock resulting from seeing or hearing the accident or its immediate aftermath.

A claim may be upheld where the claimant sees injury to others, even though he or she is in no danger, particularly where they are involved in or are responsible for the incident (*Dooley v Cammell Laird and Co* (1951); *Hunter v British Coal Corp* (1998)).

Rescuers are not to be regarded as mere bystanders and may succeed in a claim for nervous shock (*Chadwick v British*

Railways Board (1967); *Frost v Chief Constable of South Yorkshire* (1997)).

Economic loss

Economic loss arising out of physical injury or damage to property is recoverable (*Spartan Steel and Alloys Ltd v Martin and Co* (1973); *London Waste v Amec* (1997)). However, pure economic loss is not (*Murphy v Brentwood DC* (1990)), unless it is as the result of a negligent misstatement.

Negligent misstatements

A defendant may be liable for economic loss resulting from a negligent misstatement where a special relationship is established between the defendant and the claimant (*Hedley Byrne and Co v Heller and Partners* (1964)). A duty of care exists in this situation where 'one party seeking information and advice is trusting the other to exercise such a degree of care as the circumstances required, where it was reasonable for him to do that and where the other party gave the information or advice when he knew or ought to have known the inquirer was relying on him'.

There may be concurrent liability in tort and contract for such statements (*Henderson v Merritt Syndicates Ltd* (1994)):

- there is, in general, no liability for information given on a purely social occasion;
- friends or acquaintances utilising skills of their profession may be liable for negligent advice (*Chaudhry v Prabhakar* (1989));
- professionals such as accountants, lawyers and surveyors may be liable when acting in a professional capacity, although there may be limits on the extent of

their liability (*Caparo Industries plc v Dickman* (1990); *White v Jones* (1995); *Smith v Eric Bush* and *Harris Wyre Forest District Council* (1989)).

Breach of duty of care

Once the claimant has established that the defendant owes him a duty of care, he must then establish that the defendant is in breach of this duty. A breach occurs if the defendant:

> ... fails to do something which a reasonable man guided upon those considerations which ordinarily regulate the conduct of human affairs would do, or does something which a prudent and reasonable man would not do [*Blyth v Birmingham Water Works Co* (1856)].

In establishing a breach of duty the following factors are relevant:

- the likelihood of injury: the greater the risk of injury the higher the standard of care (*Bolton v Stone* (1951));
- knowledge about the claimant (*Paris v Stepney BC* (1951));
- cost and practicability: if the cost of taking precautions far outweighs the risk, the standard of care will have been satisfied (*Latimer v AEC Ltd* (1952));
- social utility: the degree of risk has to be balanced against the social utility and importance of the defendant's activity (*Watt v Hertfordshire CC* (1954));
- common practice: as long as the common practice is not inherently negligent, the standard of care may be satisfied;
- skilled persons: the actions of the skilled person must be judged against the ordinary skilled man in that particular job or profession (*Bolam v Friern HMC* (1957));

↻ *res ipsa loquitur*: whilst the burden of proof normally rests on the claimant, negligence may be inferred from the facts. This will occur where the only explanation for what happened is the negligence of the defendant, yet the claimant has insufficient evidence to establish the defendant's negligence in the normal way. The following criteria must be satisfied:

- the defendant must have had sole management or control of the thing causing the damage;
- the occurrence could not have happened without negligence (*Widdowson v Newgate Meat Corp* (1997));
- the cause of the occurrence is unknown (*Pearson v NW Gas Board* (1968)). The defendant can rebut the presumption of negligence by providing a satisfactory explanation.

Causation

The claimant must then show that 'but for' the defendant's actions the damage would not have happened – this is known as causation in fact. If the same result would have occurred regardless of the breach, then it is unlikely that the breach caused the injury (*Barnett v Chelsea and Kensington HMC* (1969)):

↻ the defendant's breach must be a material contributory cause of the injury (*Wilsher v Essex AHA* (1988));

↻ where there are successive tortfeasors, the courts will have to decide how far each one is responsible for the damage caused (*Baker v Willoughby* (1970));

↻ a *novus actus interveniens* (new intervening act) may break the chain of causation, allowing the defendant to

avoid liability for damage caused after the breach. There
are three recognised categories of *novus actus*:

- unforeseen natural event (*Carslogie Steamship Co
  Ltd v Royal Norwegian Government* (1952));
- the act of a third party (*Lamb v Camden LBC*
  (1981));
- the act of the claimant (*McKew v Holland Hannan
  and Cubbits (Scotland) Ltd* (1969)).

Remoteness of damage

Even where causation is established, the defendant will only
be liable for damage which is reasonably foreseeable. If the
type of harm is foreseen, the defendant will be liable (*The
Wagon Mound (No 1)* (1961); *Hughes v Lord Advocate*
(1963); *Doughty v Turner Manufacturing Co Ltd* (1964)).

However, if the harm is foreseeable, the defendant will be
liable even where the claimant has some weakness or
susceptibility (*Smith v Leech Brain & Co* (1961); *Robinson v
Post Office* (1974)).

Defences

The liability of the defendant may be reduced or limited by the
following:

- contributory negligence: this occurs where the claimant is
  found to have contributed in some way to his injury;
- *volenti non fit injuria* (consent): this may be a defence
  where the claimant is found to have freely assented to
  the risk of a tort being committed.

12 Employers' liability

Employers' liability is a negligence-based tort. Employers are, therefore, under a duty to take reasonable care for the safety of their employees whilst they are at work. An injured employee who wishes to pursue an action based on the liability of his employer must establish the following:

- duty of care;
- breach of duty of care;
- causation and resultant damage.

Duty of care

The employer's duty of care is owed to each individual employee. It is a personal duty and is non-delegable (*Wilsons and Clyde Coal Co v English* (1938)).

The duty is owed whilst the employee is acting within the course of his employment (*Davidson v Handley-Page Ltd* (1945)).

The employer's duty extends to the following:

- the provision of competent fellow employees (*O'Reilly v National Rail and Tramway Appliances Ltd* (1966); *Hudson v Ridge Manufacturing Co Ltd* (1957));
- the provision and maintenance of safe plant and appliances (*Bradford v Robinson Rentals Ltd* (1967)): see also the Employers' Liability (Defective Equipment) Act 1969, which provides that the employer will be deemed to be negligent for defective equipment supplied by a third party;
- the provision of a safe place of work: this includes any premises under the control of the employer including

access and egress (*Wilson v Tyneside Window Cleaning Co* (1958); *Smith v Vange Scaffolding and Engineering Co Ltd* (1970));

the provision of a safe system of work: this extends to the physical layout of the job, training, supervision, safe working practices. It also encompasses claims for stress at work and work related upper limb disorders (*Pickford v Imperial Chemical Industries plc* (1998); *Walker v Northumberland CC* (1994); *King v Smith* (1995)).

Breach of duty

The claimant must establish that the employer failed to act as a reasonable employer. The standard of care is subject to the following:

the likelihood of injury (*Paris v Stepney BC* (1951));
egg-shell skull rule (*James v Hepworth and Grandage Ltd* (1968));
the nature of the hazard balanced against the risk of injury (*Hawkins v Ian Ross (Castings) Ltd* (1970)).

Causation and resultant damage

As with claims for negligence, the claimant must satisfy the 'but for' test and also show that the damage was reasonably foreseeable (*Doughty v Turner Manufacturing* (1964); *Smith v Leech Brain and Co* (1962); see also Chapter 11).

Standards imposed by statute

Statute may introduce responsibilities on the employer which go beyond the issue of 'reasonableness'. For example, the Provision and Use of Work Equipment Regulations 1992 impose strict liability on the employer for injury caused by defective tools and equipment – such liability is not fault-based. See *Stark v Post Office* (2000).

Vicarious liability

An employer will be vicariously liable for torts committed by his employee whilst that employee is acting within the course of his employment. The claimant must, however, establish the following:

- an employer/employee relationship;
- the commission of a tort by the employee;
- the commission of the tort whilst the employee was either carrying out his or her job, or carrying out something reasonably incidental to that job (*Century Insurance Co Ltd v Northern Ireland Road Transport Board* (1942));
- a prohibited act done for the purpose of the employer's business may still result in the employee being within the course of employment (*Rose v Plenty* (1976));
- an employer may not, however, be liable for an unforeseen act which is deemed to be a 'frolic of one's own' (*Harrison v Michelin Tyre Co Ltd* (1985); *Heasmans v Clarity Cleaning Co Ltd* (1987));
- the employer may be liable for a breach of a position of trust on the part of the employee (*Morris v Martin and Sons Ltd* (1966); *Lloyd v Grace, Smith and Co* (1912)).

13 Employment: rights

A wide range of employment rights are available to employees, at least in theory.

Contract of employment

The relationship between the employee and the employer is governed by the contract of employment, which forms the basis of the employee's employment rights. Employees are employed under a contract of employment or contract of service, whereas self-employed persons are employed under a contract for services. The following tests enable the court to distinguish between the two types of contract:

(a) **Control test**

An employer should control not only what the employee does but how he does it (*Walker v Crystal Palace FC* (1910)).

(b) **Integration test**

An employee will be fully integrated into the employer's business, whereas an independent contractor does not become part of the employer's business (*Stevenson, Jordan and Harrison Ltd v MacDonald and Evans* (1952); *Whittaker v Minister of Pensions and National Insurance* (1967); *Cassidy v Minister of Health* (1951)).

(c) **Multiple test**

This considers factors in a contract which are consistent with the existence of a contract of employment. The following conditions should be fulfilled:

● that the employee provides his own work and skill in return for a wage or remuneration; if this is by way of a contract, it may give rise to the necessary mutuality of obligation required by the House of Lords in *Carmichael v National Power plc* (1999);

⊃ that the employee is under a sufficient degree of control of the employer;

⊃ that the other provisions of the contract are consistent with the existence of a contract of service (*Ready Mixed Concrete (South East) Ltd v Minister of Pensions and National Insurance* (1968); *Market Investigations Ltd v Minister of Social Security* (1969); *Hall v Lorimer* (1994)).

Other issues may include:

⊃ Who pays the income tax and national insurance?

⊃ Is the person employed entitled to holiday pay?

⊃ Who is responsible for the overall safety of the person in question (*Lane v Shire Roofing Co (Oxford) Ltd* (1995))?

⊃ What is the custom and practice of the particular industry (*Wickens v Champion Employments* (1984); *Nethermere (St Neots) v Gardiner and Tavernor* (1984))?

⊃ Can the worker provide a substitute to perform the work (*Express & Echo Publications v Tanton* (1999))?

Loaning or hiring out of employees

The presumption is that where an employee is loaned or hired out, he remains the employee of the first employer (*Mersey Docks and Harbour Board v Coggins and Griffiths (Liverpool) Ltd* (1947)). However, the presumption can be rebutted (*Sime v Sutcliffe Catering* (1990)).

'Employee' is defined in the Employment Rights Act (ERA) 1996 as an individual who has entered into, or works under, a contract of employment (s 230(1)).

Formation of the contract of employment

With regard to contracts of employment:

a) they can be made orally or in writing, with the exception of apprenticeship deeds and articles for merchant seamen;

b) the employer must provide written particulars of the main terms within two months of the date on which employment commenced (Pt 1 of the ERA 1996). The particulars must contain the following:

- names of the parties;
- date on which employment commenced;
- rate of pay or method of calculating it;
- intervals at which wages are to be paid;
- terms and conditions relating to hours of work;
- terms and conditions relating to holidays and holiday pay;
- length of notice;
- job title and description;
- place of work;
- any collective agreement directly affecting the terms and conditions;
- details of any work to be carried on outside the UK.

The written particulars must also refer to the following documents:

- the disciplinary rules;
- the disciplinary procedure;
- the grievance procedure;
- rights relating to sick pay and pensions scheme.

Express terms

These are terms agreed between the employer and employee on entering the contract of employment.

Implied terms

These arise out of custom and practice of a particular industry. Additionally, there are a number of terms implied or imposed by statute, eg an equality clause imposed by the Equal Pay Act 1970.

Duties imposed on the employer

(a) **To provide work**
   The employer should provide the employee with the opportunity to work, or if no work is available, then this duty may be satisfied by the payment of wages (*Devonald v Rosser and Sons* (1986); *Collier v Sunday Referee Publishing Co Ltd* (1940)).

(b) **To pay wages**
   Every employee is entitled to an itemised pay statement showing gross salary, deductions and net salary. Any deductions from wages must either be authorised by statute or by a provision in the employee's contract. The employer must pay his employees' wages even if there is no work available.

(c) **To indemnify the employee**

(d) **To treat an employee with mutual respect**
   See *Donovan v Evicta Airways Ltd* (1970); *WA Goold Pearmak Ltd v McConnell and Another* (1995).

(e) **To provide for the care and safety of the employee**
   See Chapter 12.

Duties imposed on the employee

The duties of the employee are to:

- obey lawful and reasonable orders (*Pepper v Webb* (1969));
- act faithfully (*Faccenda Chicken Ltd v Fowler* (1986); *Nova Plastics Ltd v Froggatt* (1982); *Hivac Ltd v Park Royal Scientific Instruments Ltd* (1946); *Adamson v B and L Cleaning Services Ltd* (1995));
- use skill and care in the performance of his job (*Lister v Romford Ice and Cold Storage Co Ltd* (1957));
- not take bribes or make a secret profit (*Sinclair v Neighbour* (1967); *Reading v AG* (1951)).

Equal pay

Legislation governing equal pay:

- Art 141 (formerly Art 119) of the EC Treaty;
- Directive 75/117;
- Equal Pay Act (EPA)1970.

An equality clause which has the effect of equalising terms and conditions in a man and woman's contract of employment is implied into all contracts of employment (s 1(1) of the EPA).

Under Art 141, 'pay' includes 'any consideration in cash or in kind', eg, sick pay (*Rinner-Kuhn v FWW Spezial-Gebäudereinigung* (1989)); concessionary travel (*Garland v British Rail Engineering Ltd* (1982)).

Each term of the contract should be considered individually, and where less favourable than the comparative term, it should be equalised (*Hayward v Cammell Laird Shipbuilders Ltd* (1988)).

Claiming equality

The applicant must show:

- employment under a contract of service or under a contract for services (s 1(6) of the EPA; *Mirror Group Newspapers Ltd v Gunning* (1986));
- employment by the same employer at the same establishment, or by the same employer or an associated employer at an establishment where common terms and conditions are observed (s 1(6); *Leverton v Clwyd CC* (1989); *British Coal Corp v Smith* (1996), which concluded that common terms and conditions meant terms and conditions which are comparable substantially on a broad basis);
- the comparator is of the opposite sex;
- the comparator may be a predecessor (*McCarthys v Smith* (1980));
- the comparator may be a successor (*Diocese of Hallam Trustee v Connaughton* (1996)).

Grounds of claim

Grounds of claim include:

(a) Like work (s 1(2)(a) of the EPA)

An applicant may claim like work where they are employed on the same work or work of a broadly similar nature as their comparator (s 1(4) of the EPA; *Capper Pass Ltd v Lawton* (1977)):

- differences of practical importance cannot be ignored (*Eaton Ltd v Nuttall* (1977));

- the time at which work is done is generally irrelevant (*Dugdale v Kraft Foods Ltd* (1977); *Thomas v NCB* (1987));
- what is actually done in practice, rather than in theory, will be considered (*Shields v Coomes (Holdings) Ltd* (1978)).

(b) Work rated equivalent (s 1(2)(b) of the EPA)

An applicant may bring a claim where her job has been rated as equivalent to that of her male comparator under a job evaluation scheme (*Bromley v H and J Quick Ltd* (1988); *Eaton Ltd v Nuttall* (1977)).

(c) Equal value

The work of equal value provision allows the applicant to claim the same pay as her male comparator if she is doing work of the same value in terms of the demands made on her (s 1(2)(c) of the EPA):

- an equal value claim may be made, even though there is a man employed in the same job as the woman (*Pickstone v Freemans plc* (1988));
- in determining whether work is of equal value, the employment tribunal (ET) tends to take a broad brush approach (*Pickstone v Freemans plc* (1993));
- work of a higher value to the comparator is also covered by an equal value claim (*Murphy v Bord Telecom Eireann* (1988));
- the procedure in equal value claims is complex (see the following diagram).

Procedure for equal value cases

DIRECTIONS HEARING

INITIAL HEARING

Are there reasonable grounds for determining that the work is of equal value?

Consideration of the material factor defence

Should the claim be referred to an independent expert, or can the IT determine the outcome itself?

REFERENCE TO AN INDEPENDENT EXPERT

The IE will determine whether the work of the woman and the man is of equal value

Provide a date by which the IE will report to the IT

FOLLOWING THE IE'S REPORT, THE HEARING IS RESUMED

Genuine material factor defence

This defence allows the employer to prove that the variation in pay is genuinely due to a material factor which is not based on the difference in the sex of the applicant and her comparator. This is an objective test.

The burden of proof is on the applicant to establish that his or her work falls within either the like work, work rated equivalent, or work of equal value provisions.

The employer may raise the genuine material difference/factor defence either at the preliminary hearing or at the full hearing, although it can no longer be pleaded at both.

The following may amount to a genuine material difference/factor:

- red circled agreements: these allow the employer to protect an employee's or group of employees' salaries, even though he or they may have been moved to a lower grade of work (*Snoxall v Vauxhall Motors Ltd* (1977));
- different geographical areas (*NAAFI v Varley* (1977));
- seniority and experience (*Nimz v Freie und Hansestadt Hamburg* (1991));
- market forces (*Rainey v Greater Glasgow Health Board* (1987));
- factors not tainted by discrimination (*Strathclyde Regional Council v Wallace* (1998)).

The following may not be a defence to a claim for equal pay:

- compulsory competitive tendering (*Ratcliffe v North Yorkshire CC* (1995));
- collective bargaining and separate pay structures (*British Coal Corp v Smith* (1996); *British Road Services v Loughrin* (1997));
- a lack of transparency in pay systems may defeat the genuine material difference defence (*Handels -og*

Kontorfunktionaerernes Forbund i Danmark v Dansk Arbejdsgiverforening (acting for Danfoss) (1989)).

Remedies

Remedies include compensation: although the Equal Pay Act 1970 set a two year limitation period for claiming arrears following the ECJ decision in *Levez v PH Jennings (Harlow Pools) Ltd* (1999) a six year limitation now applies.

Sex, race and disability discrimination

Sources

Provisions regarding sex, race and disability discrimination are to be found in:

- Directive 76/207; Sex Discrimination Act (SDA)1975;
- Race Relations Act (RRA)1976;
- Disability Discrimination Act (DDA)1995.

Who is protected?

The legislation covers anyone intending to be employed under a contract of employment.

Types of unlawful discrimination

Discrimination is unlawful if it is based upon:

- sex/gender;
- racial grounds/group;
- marital status;
- disability;
- religion or belief.

The definition of 'racial grounds' is to be found in s 3(1) of the RRA. This is defined as any of the following:

- colour;
- race;
- nationality;
- ethnic or national origins (*Northern Joint Police Board v Power* (1997); *Dawkins v Department of the Environment* (1993)).

The test for establishing 'ethnic origin' can be found in *Mandla v Dowell Lee* (1983)).

The relevant characteristics are:

- a long shared history;
- a cultural tradition;
- a common geographical area;
- descent from a number of common ancestors;
- a common language;
- a common literature;
- a common religion;
- being a minority or being an oppressed or dominant group within the larger community.

Direct discrimination

Direct discrimination covers both overt and covert acts against the individual. The test for establishing direct discrimination was established in *R v Birmingham CC ex p EOC* (1989); supported by the decision in *James v Eastleigh BC* (1990).

The test is as follows:

- Has there been an act of discrimination?
- If the answer is in the affirmative, but for the sex, race or disability of the complainant, would he or she have been treated more favourably?

The intention of the discriminator is irrelevant (*Grieg Community Industry* (1996)).

Direct discrimination may be inferred from the facts of the case if the employer cannot provide a legitimate reason for his actions (*Noone v North West Thames RHA* (1988)).

The RRA recognises transferred discrimination. For example, if a white barmaid is instructed to refuse to serve black people, and on refusing to do so is dismissed, she can claim direct discrimination under the RRA (*Zarcynska v Levy* (1978); *Weatherfield Ltd t/a Van and Truck Rentals v Sargent* (1998)).

Sexual and racial harassment

Note that:

- harassment is a form of direct discrimination;
- there are no separate provisions concerning sexual harassment in the legislation;
- harassment includes any conduct meted out in a particular way because of the complainant's gender, race or disability. It is not confined to conduct of a purely physical nature (*Strathclyde RDC v Porcelli* (1986));
- a single act may amount to harassment if it is of a serious nature (*Bracebridge Engineering v Darby* (1990)); a single verbal comment may amount to harassment if it is sufficiently serious (*In Situ Cleaning v Heads* (1995)).
- racial or sexual insults may amount to harassment (*De Souza v Automobile Association* (1986));
- the complainant must establish that they have suffered a detriment (*De Souza v Automobile Association* (1986));
- the EC Resolution relating to sexual harassment at work (Resolution 6015/90) has led to a recommendation and code of practice on the protection and dignity of women and men at work. It is expected that the ET will consider

the employer's application of the code of practice in any harassment cases (*Wadman v Carpenter Farrer Partnership* (1993));

employers will be vicariously liable for acts of harassment committed by their employees unless they have taken all reasonable precautions to prevent such acts;

in considering whether an employee is within the course of his employment when he commits an act of harassment, the courts have adopted a purposive construction of s 32 of the RRA and s 41 of the SDA so as to deter acts of harassment in the workplace (*Tower Boot Co Ltd v Jones* (1997));

s 4A of the Public Order Act 1986 provides for the offence of intentional harassment, involving the use of threatening, abusive or insulting words or behaviour causing another person harassment, alarm or distress;

the Protection from Harassment Act 1997 creates a criminal offence and a statutory tort of harassment.

Pregnancy

With regard to pregnancy:

discrimination against a pregnant woman or a woman on maternity leave may constitute direct discrimination (*Webb v EMO Cargo Ltd (No 2)* (1994); *Brown v Rentokil Initial UK Ltd* (1998));

the protected period extends to the end of the maternity leave period. However, comparison with how a sick man would have been treated is legitimate outside this period (*Handels -og Kontorfunktionaerernes Forbund i Danmark (acting for Hertz) v Dansk Arbejdsgiverforening* (1991); *British Telecommunications plc v Roberts and Longstaff* (1996));

⊃ protection for the pregnancy and maternity leave perio
applies not only to permanent contracts but also arguab
to fixed term contracts (*Caruana v Manchester Airport p*
(1996));

⊃ it is automatically unfair to dismiss a woman for a reaso
connected with her pregnancy (*Caledonia Burea
Investment and Property v Caffrey* (1998); ERA 1996)).

Indirect discrimination

Indirect discrimination is conduct which, on the face of it, doe
not treat people differently, ie, it is race and gender neutra
However, it is the impact of this treatment which amounts t
discrimination. In order to prove discrimination the followin
must be established:

⊃ a requirement or condition applied equally to both sexe
and/or racial groups (*Price v Civil Service Commissio*
(1977); *Falkirk Council v Whyte* (1997));

⊃ a considerably smaller proportion of the complainant'
sex or race can comply with it compared to the opposit
sex or persons not of that racial group (*Londo
Underground Ltd v Edwards (No 2)* (1997); *Pearse v Ci
of Bradford Metropolitan Council* (1988));

⊃ the requirement or condition operates to the detriment c
the complainant because he or she cannot comply with
(*Clarke v Eley (IMI) Kynock Ltd* (1972));

⊃ the requirement or condition can be justified irrespectiv
of the gender or race of the complainant;

⊃ the burden of proof is initially on the complainan
however, it moves to the employer to show justificatior
The test is an objective one, in which the employer mus
show a real need on the part of the undertaking to operat
the practice, which is then balanced against th
discriminatory impact of the practice (*Hampson*

Department of Science (1989)); the EC Burden of Proof Directive will move the burden of proof onto the employer.

Victimisation

This is a separate form of discrimination (s 2 of the RRA; s 4 of the SDA):

- the complainant must show that he or she has been treated less favourably by reason that he or she has brought proceedings against the discriminator or another person under the RRA, SDA, EPA or DDA.
- it extends to the giving of evidence or information in connection with proceedings brought by another person;
- the complainant must show a clear connection between the action of the discriminator and his or her own conduct (*Aziz v Trinity Street Taxis Ltd* (1988)).

Segregation

Remember that:

- segregation is only applicable to racial discrimination;
- providing separate facilities for members of different races, even if they are equal in quality, is unlawful (s 1(2) of the RRA; *Pel Ltd v Modgill* (1980)).

Scope of protection

Once the complainant has established the type of discrimination, he or she must show how this relates to s 6 of the SDA, s 4 of the RRA, or s 4 of the DDA, which have the effect of making the act of discrimination unlawful.

Discrimination is unlawful if it occurs in the following situations:

- during the selection process, including advertising selection for interview, the interview process;
- during the period of employment;
- the provision of opportunities during employment, e training, promotion or other benefits;
- the dismissal of employees or subjecting them to an other detriment.

Genuine occupational qualification

Both s 7 of the SDA and s 5 of the RRA permit discrimination by an employer if it falls within specified genuine occupation. qualifications. These include the following:

- the nature of the job demands a man or woman becaus of their physiology, excluding strength and stamina;
- authenticity;
- decency or privacy (*Lasertop Ltd v Webster* (1997));
- the post requires the employee to live in where there an no separate sleeping or sanitary facilities and it unreasonable to expect the employer to provide them;
- a post in a private home;
- the holder of the post supplies individuals or persons of particular race with personal services promoting the welfare, education, etc (*Tottenham Green Under Five Centre v Marshall (No 2)* (1991));
- a post which involves working abroad in a country whos laws and customs are such that the job can only be don by a man;
- the job is one of two which are held by a married coupl

Bringing a claim

A claim must be brought within three months of the date c which the act complained of was committed.

Remedies

For sex and race discrimination:

- unlimited compensation is available;
- the ET may make a declaration with respect to the rights of the complainant;
- the ET may make a recommendation for the employer to take specific action with respect to the act of discrimination.

Disability discrimination

The DDA 1995 mirrors the direct discrimination provisions of the SDA and RRA. There are, however, the following limitations:

- the DDA only applies to employers who employ 15 or more employees;
- the employer is provided with a justification defence to less favourable treatment (s 5 of the DDA);
- 'disabled' is defined in the Disability Discrimination (Meaning of Disability) Regulations 1996 – it includes physical or mental impairment which has a substantial and long term adverse effect on his/her ability to carry out normal day to day activities.

However, the employer is under an additional duty to make adjustments to premises to ensure that the disabled person is not placed at a substantial disadvantage in comparison with persons who are not disabled (s 6 of the DDA). The employer is provided with a justification defence if he can show that the cost and nature of the adjustments as well as the practicability of making them is unreasonable.

14 Employment: termination and dismissal

Termination

Termination of the contract of employment may occur in a number of ways:

- death;
- mutual agreement;
- expiry of fixed term contract;
- frustration;
- dismissal.

Dismissal

Where an employer terminates the employee's contract, a minimum period of notice should be given. The period of notice will either be that stated in the contract of employment, or in s 86 of the ERA 1996. The period of notice is as follows:

- employment between one month and two years – one week's notice;
- employment for more than two years – one week's notice for each year of employment, subject to a maximum of 12 weeks (s 86);
- either party may waive their right to notice;
- wages or salary may be provided in lieu of notice;
- an employee may be dismissed without notice for serious misconduct.

Wrongful dismissal

- This is a common law action;
- available to those who do not qualify under the ERA 199
  for an unfair dismissal action;
- available to an employee who has been dismisse
  unjustifiably without notice;
- the calculation of damages is subject to the law o
  contract (*Dietman v Brent LBC* (1988));
- other remedies, such as injunctions, may be availabl
  (*Irani v South West Hampshire HA* (1985); *Powell
  London Borough of Brent* (1987); *Anderson v Pringle o
  Scotland Ltd* (1998)) but specific performance is no
  available.

Unfair dismissal

The ERA 1996 provides protection for those unfairl
dismissed from their employment.

Who qualifies:

- all those employed under a contract of service; and
- those with at least one year's continuous employmen
  (after a minimum of one year's continuous service).

The following are specifically excluded:

- share fishermen;
- any employee who has reached the normal retiremen
  age;
- employees who, at the time of their dismissal, are takin
  industrial action or are locked out and there has been n
  selective dismissal or re-engagement of those takin
  part;

🔁 where the settlement for the claim for dismissal has been agreed with the involvement of ACAS (the Advisory, Conciliation and Arbitration Service) and the employee has agreed to withdraw his or her complaint.

Effective date of termination

With regard to the termination of contracts of employment:

🔁 any claim must be brought within three months of the effective date of termination;

🔁 the date of termination is the date on which the notice expires (*Adams v GKN Sankey* (1980));

🔁 where no notice is given, the date of termination is the date on which the termination takes effect (*Robert Cort and Sons Ltd v Charman* (1981));

🔁 where a contract is for a fixed term, the date of termination is the date on which the term expires.

What is meant by dismissal?

The onus is on the employee to show that he or she has been dismissed within the meaning of s 95 of the ERA 1996. Dismissal may occur in the following ways:

🔁 express termination of the contract of employment by the employer;

🔁 if the words used are ambiguous, the ET will assess whether the reasonable employer or employee would have understood the words to be tantamount to dismissal (*Futty v Brekkes Ltd* (1974));

🔁 termination by mutual agreement does not amount to dismissal. However, the ET will consider such cases very carefully (*Igbo v Johnson Matthey Chemicals Ltd* (1986));

- inviting the employee to resign may amount to dismissal (*Robertson v Securicor Transport Ltd* (1972));
- expiration of a fixed term contract. If a fixed term contract is not renewed and is not within the excluded category, failure to renew amounts to a dismissal.

Constructive dismissal

Constructive dismissal arises where the employee is forced to terminate the contract, with or without notice, due to the conduct of the employer:

- the employer's actions must amount to breach of contract to warrant the employee taking this action (*Western Excavating Ltd v Sharp* (1978));
- the breach must go to the root of the contract (*British Aircraft Corp v Austin* (1978));
- if the employee does not resign in the event of the breach by the employer, he will be deemed to have accepted the breach and waived any rights (*Cox Toner (International) Ltd v Krug* (1981));
- a series of minor incidents may have a cumulative effect resulting in a fundamental breach (*Woods v WM Car Services (Peterborough)* (1982));
- a breach of an implied term may also allow the employee to claim constructive dismissal (*Gardener Ltd v Beresford* (1978); *Vaid v Brintel Helicopters Ltd* (1994)).

Written statements of the reason for dismissal

Where an employee has been dismissed within the meaning of the ERA 1996, he is entitled to a written statement of the reasons for his dismissal, subject to the following:

- continuous employment for one year;
- employee must request the statement;
- it must be supplied within 14 days of the request;
- failure to provide the statement will allow the employee to make a complaint to an ET;
- an award of two weeks' pay may be made if the written statement has been wrongfully withheld.

Fair dismissals

Once the employee has established that a dismissal has taken place, the onus is on the employer to show that he or she has acted reasonably in dismissing the employee, and therefore that the dismissal is fair (s 98 of the ERA 1996). The test of reasonableness is as follows: has the employer acted as a reasonable employer in all the circumstances (*Iceland Frozen Foods v Jones* (1982); *Polkey v AE Dayton Services Ltd* (1987))?

The following factors will be considered by the ET:

- length of service;
- previous disciplinary record;
- any other mitigating circumstances, such as use of disciplinary procedures (*Cabaj v Westminster CC* (1996)).

The employer must act reasonably and, therefore, must consider any possible alternatives if the dismissal is to be regarded as fair.

Additionally the tribunal will consider issues of procedure: the lack of fair procedure may render an otherwise fair dismissal unfair (*Polkey v AE Dayton Services Ltd* (1987)). Section 34 of the Employment Act 2002 introduces a statutory disciplinary procedure which should be adhered to by all parties; however, failure to follow the procedure will not necessarily render the dismissal unfair.

The following grounds are potentially fair reasons for dismissal (s 98 of the ERA 1996):

(a) Capability or qualifications

When considering the employee's capabilities or qualifications, the following must be taken into account:

- 'capability' means skill, aptitude, health or any other physical or mental quality;
- 'qualification' means any degree, diploma or other academic, technical or professional qualification relevant to the position which the employee held (*Blackman v Post Office* (1974));
- the employer should attempt to improve poor performance before dismissing an employee (*Davison v Kent Motors Ltd* (1975));
- appropriate warning should be provided unless the act of incompetence is so serious that warnings are inappropriate (*Taylor v Alidair* (1978));
- long term sickness should be properly investigated before a dismissal takes place (*London Fire and Civil Defence Authority v Betty* (1994)).

(b) Conduct

Whether dismissal for misconduct is fair will depend on:

- the nature of the defence and the appropriate use of the disciplinary procedure (*Hamilton v Argyll and Clyde Health Board* (1993)). Reasonable investigation should be carried out by the employer into the conduct (*Robinson v Crompton Parkinson Ltd* (1978));
- the employer must act as a reasonable employer (*Taylor v Parsons Peebles Ltd* (1981));

◯ where it is impossible to ascertain which employee is guilty where a number are implicated, it may be reasonable to dismiss all the employees concerned (*Parr v Whitbread plc* (1990); *Whitbread and Co v Thomas* (1988)).

(c) Redundancy

Redundancy may amount to a fair dismissal subject to the following:

◯ sufficient warning;
◯ consultation with the trade union;
◯ adoption of objective rather than subjective criteria for selection;
◯ selection in accordance with the criteria;
◯ redeployment rather than dismissal where possible (*Williams v Compair Maxam Ltd* (1982));
◯ where selection for redundancy was because the employee was a member or non-member of a trade union or participated in trade union activities, this will automatically be unfair dismissal (s 153 of the Trade Union and Labour Relations (Consolidation) Act 1992 (TULRCA)).

(d) Statutory restrictions

Where the continued employment of the employee would result in a contravention of a statute or subordinate legislation, the dismissal will be *prima facie* fair (*Fearn v Tayford Motor Co Ltd* (1975)).

(e) Some other substantial reason

There is no exhaustive list of what amounts to other substantial reason. The following are examples:

- ⮑ conflict of personalities, primarily the fault of the employee (*Tregeanowan v Robert Knee and Co* (1975));
- ⮑ failure to disclose material facts in obtaining employment (*O'Brien v Prudential Assurance Co Ltd* (1979));
- ⮑ failure to accept changes in the terms of employment (*Storey v Allied Brewery* (1977));
- ⮑ a dismissal which satisfies reg 8(2) of the Transfer of Undertakings (Protection of Employment) Regulations 1981 in so far as the dismissal is for an 'economic, technical or organisational reason entailing changes in the workforce and the employer is able to show that his actions were reasonable'.

Situations where the dismissal is automatically unfair

Dismissal on the following grounds is automatically unfair:

- ⮑ trade union membership or activities (s 152 of TULRCA);
- ⮑ pregnancy or childbirth (s 99 of the ERA 1996): a dismissal is automatically unfair if the principal reason for it is pregnancy or a reason connected with pregnancy, or following the maternity leave period, dismissal for childbirth or a reason connected with childbirth (*O'Neill v Governors of Saint Thomas More RCVA School* (1996));
- ⮑ industrial action: dismissal of those participating in an official strike, lock-out or other official industrial action will be unfair if only some of the participants are dismissed or if all are dismissed but only some are offered re-engagement within a three month period (s 238 of TULRCA); dismissal of workers participating in lawful

official industrial action will be unfair if within the first eight weeks of the action (or longer if the employer has failed to take reasonable steps to resolve the action) (s 238A of TULRCA 1992).

- industrial pressure: where an employer dismisses an employee because of industrial pressure from other employees, the dismissal may be unfair (s 107 of the ERA 1996);
- s 100 of the ERA 1996 provides that an employee has the right not to be dismissed for carrying out health and safety activities, drawing health and safety matters to the attention of the employer, or taking appropriate steps to protect him or herself or other persons from danger, including leaving the workplace or refusing to return to the workplace (*Harries v Select Timber Frame Ltd* (1994); *Lopez v Maison Bouquillon Ltd* (1996)).

Remedies

Remedies include:

- reinstatement;
- re-engagement;
- compensation:
  - basic award, calculated on the basis of age and continuous service;
  - compensatory award – discretionary;
  - additional award – for failing to comply with an order for reinstatement or re-engagement;
  - special award – where dismissal relates to trade union membership;
  - interim relief.

Redundancy

Where an employee's services are no longer required by the business, the employee may be entitled to redundancy payments. The employee must show:

- continuous employment for a period of two years;
- employment under a contract of service;
- that the excluded categories do not apply (see above);
- dismissal and the reason for dismissal was redundancy.

Redundancy defined (s 139 of the ERA 1996)

The following amount to redundancy situations:

- cessation of the employer's business;
- closure or change in the place of work. Moving to new premises in the same town may not amount to redundancy (*Managers (Holburn) Ltd v Hohne* (1997)); nor will the existence of an express mobility clause (*UK Automatic Energy Authority v Claydon* (1974));
- diminishing requirements for employees;
- lay-off and short time.

A claim for redundancy payment may be made in circumstances where the employee has been laid off or been kept on short time for either four or more consecutive weeks or for a series of six or more weeks within a period of 13 weeks. The employee must give written notice to his employer of his intention to claim redundancy payments no later than four weeks from the end of the period, and should terminate the employment by giving at least one week's notice, or the period stipulated in the contract of employment. The employer may serve a counter-notice, within seven days of the employee's notice, contesting the claim (ss 147–49 of the ERA 1996).

Change in ownership and transfer of undertaking

Continuity is preserved in the following situations:

- change of partners;
- where trustees or personal representatives take over the running of the company when the employer dies;
- transfer of employment to an associated employer;
- transfer of an undertaking, trade or business from one person to another (s 218(2) of the ERA 1996; s 33 of the Trade Union Reform and Employment Rights Act 1993).

All existing rights are transferred and become enforceable against the new business. If, following a transfer of undertaking, an employee is dismissed for an economic, technical or organisational reason, redundancy payment may be claimed (*Litster and Others v Forth Dry Dock and Engineering Co Ltd* (1989)).

Offer of alternative employment

Where the employer makes an offer of suitable alternative employment, which is unreasonably refused by the employee, the employee will be unable to claim redundancy.

Whether the alternative employment is suitable will be a question of fact in each case, by reference to the old contracts, including the place of work, nature of the work, pay and conditions, etc.

Whether a refusal by the employee is reasonable will depend, *inter alia*, on the personal circumstances of the employee (*Cambridge and District Co-Operative Society Ltd v Ruse* (1993)).

Where the employee accepts the offer of alternative employment, he is entitled to a minimum trial period of four weeks if the contract is renewed on different terms and conditions (s 132 of the ERA 1996).

Once notice of redundancy has been received, an employee is entitled to a reasonable amount of time off to seek work or retrain (s 52 of the ERA 1996).

Compensation

Redundancy pay is based on the length of service and the age of the employee.

Procedure for handling redundancies

Where redundancy is to take place, the employer should consult a recognised trade union or elected employee representative in good time. The employer must disclose the following:

- the reason for the proposed redundancies;
- the number and description of the employees whom it is proposed to make redundant;
- the total number of employees of that description employed at that establishment;
- the method of selection;
- the method of carrying out the redundancy, having regard to any procedure agreed with the trade union.

The minimum consultation periods are as follows:

- at least 90 days before the first dismissal takes effect, where the employer proposes to make 100 or more employees redundant at one establishment within a period of 90 days or less;
- at least 30 days before the first redundancy takes effect where he or she proposes to make 20 or more employees redundant at one establishment within a 30 day period.

Failure to comply with the consultation procedure may result in a protective award being made to those employees who were affected. The Secretary of State should be informed.

15 Consumer credit

Consumer Credit Act 1974

The Consumer Credit Act (CCA) 1974 applies to regulated consumer credit agreements. The key elements of such an agreement are:

- a creditor: the person or body supplying the credit or finance;
- the debtor: an individual who borrows money supplied by the creditor;
- credit: a loan not exceeding £15,000 (s 8);
- credit: token agreements may also be regulated agreements. This includes credit cards, but excludes cheque guarantee cards (s 14).

Regulated agreements may also fall within the following categories:

- restricted use credit agreement: where the debtor has no control over the use to which the credit is put;
- unrestricted use credit agreement: where the debtor has control over the use of the finance;
- debtor-creditor-supplier agreement: where there is a connection between the creditor and the supplier;
- debtor-creditor agreement: where the supplier has no connection with the person providing the credit.

Credit may be:

- fixed sum credit: where the total amount of the loan is fixed from the start of the agreement;
- running account credit: where credit is fixed up to an agreed limit, eg bank overdrafts;

 ⟳ small agreements: where the amount of credit does not exceed £50.

Licensing

Businesses which provide facilities for regulated agreements must be licensed by the Office of Fair Trading. This includes:

 ⟳ businesses whose main activity is the supply of credit;
 ⟳ businesses where the provision of credit is ancillary;
 ⟳ unlicensed traders will be unable to enforce any credit agreement;
 ⟳ trading without a licence is an offence under s 39 of the CCA 1974;
 ⟳ standard licence issued to an individual is valid for five years;
 ⟳ a group licence issued to an identifiable group is valid for 15 years.

Advertising and canvassing

Note that:

 ⟳ advertising and canvassing are controlled by the Consumer Credit (Advertisement) Regulations 1989;
 ⟳ the Regulations provide for control over the form and content of the advertisements for credit;
 ⟳ failure to comply with the Regulations is a criminal offence;
 ⟳ any advertisements should contain a fair and reasonably comprehensive indication of the nature of the credit facilities offered and their true cost;
 ⟳ canvassing off trade premises is also regulated.

Form of the regulated agreements

Consumer Credit (Agreement) Regulations 1983

If the rules affecting the form of regulated agreements are not followed, the creditor or owner will be prevented from enforcing the agreements:

- the terms of the agreement must be in writing and must be legible;
- the cash price of the goods must be stated in the agreement;
- it must provide for payment of equal instalments at equal intervals and must include reference to the method of payments;
- it must include a description of the goods sufficient to identify them;
- the agreement must contain certain statutory notices, eg right to terminate or cancel the agreement;
- it must be typewritten; there must be space for a signature in a box outlined in red.

Copies of the agreement

If the creditor or finance company signs at the same time as the hirer or debtor, then the hirer or debtor must receive a copy immediately.

If there is a time lag, then the dealer/supplier must send the forms off to the finance company for agreement and then the hirer or debtor must receive:

- a copy of his offer immediately;
- a subsequent copy of the concluded agreement within seven days.

This allows time for the debtor to be informed of his right and to withdraw from or cancel the agreement (*National Guardian Mortgage Corp v Wilkes* (1993)).

Cancellation

Note that:

- an agreement signed off trade premises is cancellable;
- the right of cancellation and the procedure to be carried out must be included in the agreement;
- the 'cooling off' period is five days from the signing of the agreement until after the second copy is received;
- goods must be returned and payments made can be recovered.

Default

Where a debtor fails to meet the repayments, the goods can normally be repossessed.

Where the goods are deemed to be protected goods, ie, the debtor has paid one-third or more of the price, the owner of the goods can only enforce his right to repossess the goods by court action.

Repossession without a court order will result in termination of the agreement and the debtor will be able to claim back any money he has paid under the agreement.

Where a court order is obtained, the court may order the return of the goods to the owner or may order a variation of the terms of the original agreement, or may order part of the goods to be transferred to the debtor.

Before any action for repossession can be pursued, the owner or creditor must serve a default notice on the hirer or debtor giving the hirer or debtor seven days' notice to pay or remedy the default.

Following receipt of a default notice, the debtor or hirer may apply for a time order from the court which allows him extra time to make payments or rectify the breach (*Southern District Finance v Barnes* (1995)).

Termination of regulated agreements

Where there is a regulated hire purchase or conditional sale agreement, the debtor can terminate at any time, provided notice is given to the finance company or its agent. The debtor or hirer may be required to pay up to 50% of the price of the goods as well as all sums due.

Extortionate credit bargains

If a credit agreement is deemed to be extortionate by the court, the court may reopen the agreement and either set it aside or rewrite the terms (*Ketley Ltd v Scott* (1981)).

Credit reference agencies

A person who has been refused credit may request the name and address of the credit reference agency from the creditor.

On receipt of a written request, the agency must supply a copy of the customer's file which the customer can then apply to have amended.

16 Sale of goods

Sources

- Sale of Goods Act (SGA)1979;
- Sale and Supply of Goods Act 1994;
- Sale of Goods (Amendment) Acts 1994 and 1995;
- Supply of Goods and Services Act 1982.

The definition of a contract for the sale of goods

This is defined as a 'contract by which the seller transfers or agrees to transfer the property in goods to the buyer for money consideration called the price' (s 2(1) of the SGA):

- consideration must be in monetary form;
- the price is to be fixed by the contract or determined by the course of dealings between the parties;
- 'goods include personal property of a movable type' – land and buildings are specifically excluded;
- any agreement can be made orally or in writing.

Transfer of property in the goods

Whether property in the goods can be transferred will depend on the nature of the goods. Goods can be divided into distinct categories:

- specific goods are goods identified and agreed upon at the time the contract is made;
- ascertained goods are those identified and agreed upon after the making of the contract: eg, 20 sacks of flour which are set aside for the buyer;

- unascertained goods are those which have not been specified;
- future goods are goods to be manufactured, to be acquired by the seller after the contract has been made.

The principal rules relating to the transfer of property are as follows:

- where there is a contract for the sale of unascertained goods, no property in the goods is transferred to the buyer until the goods are ascertained (s 16 of the SGA; see also s 20A);
- property passes when the parties intend to pass (s 17), subject to the general rules found in s 18: if there is a contract for specific goods, property passes to the buyer when the contract is made (s 18, r 1). The intention of the parties may overrule this (*Re Anchorline (Henderson Bros Ltd)* (1937)). For property to pass, goods must be in a deliverable state (*Dennant v Skinner and Collam* (1948));
- if there is a contract for the sale of specific goods, but the seller is bound to do something to put them in a deliverable state, then ownership does not pass until that thing is done and the buyer has notice that it is done (s 18, r 2; *Underwook v Burgh Castle Brick and Cement Syndicate* (1922));
- if the goods are to be weighed, tested or measured or subjected to some other act for the purpose of ascertaining the price, the property does not pass until the process is complete and the buyer informed (s 18, r 3);
- where goods are supplied on sale or return or on approval, property passes to the buyer when the buyer signifies approval or acceptance, or the buyer does any other act adopting the transaction, or the buyer retains the goods beyond the agreed time, or if no time is

agreed, beyond reasonable time (s 18, r 4; *Poole v Smiths Car Sales (Balham) Ltd* (1962); *Atari Corp Ltd v Electronics Boutique* (1998));

⮑ where there is a contract for the sale of unascertained or future goods by description, and goods of that description and in a deliverable state are unconditionally appropriated to the contract, either by the seller with the assent of the buyer or by the buyer with the assent of the seller, property in the goods passes to the buyer (s 18, r 5; *Carlos Federspiel and Co v Charles Twig and Co Ltd* (1957)). Goods placed with a carrier for transmission to the buyer are deemed to be unconditionally appropriated to the contract (s 18, r 5(2)). Ascertainment by exhaustion takes place where goods are part of a designated bulk and the bulk is reduced to a quantity equal to the contract quantity (*MacDougal v Eire Marine of Emsworth Ltd* (1958));

⮑ where the buyer purchases a specified quantity of goods from an identified bulk source and has paid for some or all of the goods, the buyer becomes co-owner of the bulk.

Destruction of the goods

The rules relating to the transfer of property in the goods assist in determining who is liable should the goods be destroyed or perish:

⮑ if goods perish due to delayed delivery through the fault of either the buyer or the seller, then the loss falls on the party at fault (*Demby Hamilton Co v Barden Ltd* (1949));

⮑ if the goods have perished before the contract is made, the contract is void (s 6; *Couturier v Hastie* (1956)).

If property, and therefore risk, has not been passed to the buyer when the goods perish, the contract can be avoided.

However, if risk has passed, the buyer must bear the loss (*Ashfar v Blundell* (1896)).

A seller may use a reservation of title clause to protect his interests, particularly where the buyer fails to pay for the goods. However, such clauses may impact on the transfer of property and therefore risk (*Aluminium Industrie Vaasen v Romalpa Aluminium Ltd* (1976)).

Sale by a person who is not the owner

All contracts for the sale of goods contain an implied term that the seller has the right to sell the goods, ie, that he or she can pass on good title to them (s 12). Such contracts are also subject to the rule *nemo dat quod non habet*, which means that a person cannot give what he or she has not got. This means that the rightful owner of the goods is protected. As a general rule, where goods are sold by a person who is not the owner, the buyer acquires no better title than the seller (s 21). There are, however, exceptions to that rule:

- estoppel: where the seller or buyer by their conduct make the other party believe that they have ownership in the goods and the other party alters his position, then that same party will later be estopped from saying that the fact is untrue (*Eastern Distributors v Goldring* (1957));
- agency: if a principal appoints an agent to sell his goods to a third party, then any sale by the agent in accordance with the instructions given will pass on good title to a third party (*Central Newbury Car Auctions v Unity Finance* (1957));
- mercantile agent: where the agent is a mercantile agent, ie, one who has in the customary course of business as such an agent, authority either to sell goods or to consign goods for the purpose of sale or to buy goods or to raise

money on the security of goods, a third party will obtain good title from such an agent (*Folkes v King* (1923); *Pearson v Rose and Young* (1951));

- sales authorised by law: where the sale is authorised by the courts, good title is passed to the buyer;

- sale under a voidable title: if, at the time of the sale, the seller's title has not been avoided, the buyer can acquire good title to the goods, provided that he did not know of the seller's defective title and bought the goods in good faith (s 23; *Car and Universal Finance Co v Caldwell* (1965));

- disposition by a seller in possession: if the seller sells goods to a second buyer, having retained possession of the goods, the second buyer will obtain good title if he takes the goods in good faith and without notice of the original sale. The first buyer must then sue the seller for breach of contract (*Pacific Motor Auctions v Motor Credit (Hire Finance) Ltd* (1965));

- disposition by a buyer in possession: where the buyer has possession of the goods with the consent of the seller and transfers these to an innocent second buyer, that buyer will obtain good title to the goods as long as he takes the goods in good faith and without notice of any claim on the goods by the original seller (s 25(1); *Cahn v Pockets Bristol Channel Co* (1899));

- however, if there is a reservation of title clause, the sub-purchaser may not be able to rely on s 25 (*Re Highway Foods International Ltd* (1995));

- sale of a motor vehicle subject to a hire purchase agreement – here, a private purchaser may obtain good title to the vehicle as long as he takes in good faith and without notice of the hire purchase agreement.

Implied terms

A number of terms are implied into every contract for the sale of goods. There are three types of term:

- *condition*: this is a fundamental term of the contract, any breach of which will allow the injured party to treat the contract as repudiated;
- *warranty*: this is a lesser term of the contract, a breach of which will allow the buyer to claim damages, but not to reject the goods;
- *innominate term*: this is neither a condition nor a warranty, however, a breach may result in repudiation of the contract if it is deemed to go to the root of the contract.

Title (s 12)

There is an implied condition that the seller has the right to sell the goods and the ability to transfer good title to the buyer (*Niblett Ltd v Confectioners Materials Co* (1921)).

There is an implied warranty that the goods are free from any charge or encumbrance not disclosed or known to the buyer before the contract is made, and that the buyer will have quiet possession of the goods (s 12(2); *Microbeads AC v Vinhurst Road Markings* (1975)).

Description (s 13)

Where goods are sold by description, they must accord with the description applied to them. A sale by description occurs where the buyer does not see the goods, but relies on a description of them, or where the buyer sees the goods, but relies on terms describing features of the goods or self description (*Harlingdon and Leinster Enterprises Christopher Hull Fine Art Ltd* (1990); *Beale v Taylor* (1967)).

Satisfactory quality (s 14(2))

Goods sold in the course of a business must be of satisfactory quality unless defects are specifically drawn to the buyer's attention before the contract is made, or, where the buyer examines the goods before the contract is made, any defects which that examination ought to reveal, or, in the case of contract for sale by sample, any defect which would have been apparent on reasonable examination of the sample. There is, however, no obligation on the buyer to carry out an examination. Satisfactory quality is defined as 'a standard that a reasonable person would regard as satisfactory, taking account of any description of the goods, the price if relevant and all the other relevant circumstances' (s 14(2A)). However, the quality of the goods includes their state and condition and the following (among others) are, in appropriate cases, aspects of the quality of the goods:

- fitness for all the purposes for which goods of the kind in question are commonly supplied;
- appearance and finish;
- freedom from minor defects;
- safety;
- durability (s 14(2B)).

This is a non-exhaustive list, and failure to comply with one of the factors will not necessarily result in goods being classified as unsatisfactory quality (*Rogers v Parish (Scarborough) Ltd* 1987); *Bernstein v Pamson Motors (Golders Green) Ltd* 1987)).

Reasonable fitness for the purpose

There is an implied condition that the goods supplied are reasonably fit for any purpose expressly or impliedly made known to the seller under s 14(3). If the purpose or use is unusual, or the goods have several normal but distinct uses then the purpose must be made known expressly (*Ashington Piggeries v Hill* (1972); *Griffiths v Peter Conway Ltd* (1939)).

Sale by sample (s 15)

There is an implied condition that where goods are sold by sample, they will comply with that sample. They should also be free from any defect making their quality unsatisfactory which would not be apparent on reasonable examination of the sample (*E and S Rubin v Faire Bros and Co Ltd* (1949)).

Exclusion clauses

Certain implied terms cannot be excluded:

⊃ s 12 of the SGA cannot be excluded;
⊃ ss 13–15 of the SGA cannot be excluded in a consumer sale;
⊃ ss 13–15 can only be excluded in a non-consumer sale where the test of reasonableness is satisfied.

Any other liability for breach of contract can be excluded or restricted only to the extent that it is reasonable.

Exclusion of liability for death and personal injury is prohibited (s 2(1) of UCTA).

Unfair terms in standard form consumer contracts may be challenged as being contrary to good faith (Unfair Terms in Consumer Contracts Regulations 1999).

Delivery and acceptance of the goods

It is the duty of the seller to deliver the goods and the duty of the buyer to accept them and pay for them (s 27). Payment and delivery are concurrent conditions, unless otherwise agreed (s 28):

- delivery by instalments is not acceptable unless the contract specifically states that delivery is going to take place by this method (s 31);
- the buyer may reject or accept the goods where delivery is late;
- the buyer has a right of partial rejection (s 35A).

Acceptance occurs where:

- the buyer states to the seller that the goods are acceptable;
- the goods have been delivered to the buyer and he does an act in relation to them which is inconsistent with the ownership of the seller;
- the buyer is not deemed to have accepted the goods until he has had a reasonable opportunity of examining them for the purpose of ascertaining whether they are in conformity with the contract, and in the case of a contract for sale by sample, of comparing the bulk with the sample;
- acceptance is also deemed to have taken place where the buyer retains the goods after a reasonable length of time without intimating to the seller that they will be rejected (*Bernstein v Pamson Motors (Golders Green) Ltd* (1980)).

Price

The price may be fixed or determined by an agreed procedure. The buyer must, however, pay a reasonable price, which will be a question of fact depending on the circumstances of the case (*Foley v Classique Coaches Ltd* (1934)).

Remedies for breach of contract

Seller's remedies

The seller may bring an action for the price of the goods where

- the buyer has wrongfully refused or neglected to pay for the goods according to the terms of the contract; or
- the property is passed to the buyer or the price is payable on a certain day, irrespective of delivery.

Damages for non-acceptance of the goods

The seller may pursue a claim for damages for non acceptance of the goods.

Lien

The seller has a right to retain possession of the goods, even though property is passed to the buyer where the seller remains unpaid.

Stoppage in transit

If the buyer becomes insolvent and the goods are still in transit between the seller and buyer, the unpaid seller is given the right to stop and recover the goods from the carrier.

Reservation of title clause

The insertion of such a clause in the contract allows the seller to retain some proprietary interest over the goods until payment is made by the buyer.

Right of resale

An unpaid seller can pass good title to the goods to the second buyer after exercising a right of lien or stoppage in transit.

MUSL]

CW00558076

BELIEFS AND ISSUES

KS3 TEACHER GUIDE

Pat Lunt

Badger
Publishing

Contents

Introduction

This book is part of a series on **Beliefs and Issues** which provides teaching and learning material for Key Stage 3 Religious Education. The series has been developed and written with the belief that good religious education can be seen as relevant, interesting and engaging to all students since it is concerned with studying aspects of the 'human condition'. For all of religious education there is a strong link with human experience. There are important or 'ultimate' questions that all people ask at some time in their lives. There are a number of sources for possible answers to these questions. Religions provide answers based on their own set of beliefs. It is important for students to be able to understand and appreciate views, opinions and beliefs other than their own in today's world of secularism, multi-culturalism and religious diversity.

The material seeks to:

- identify the link between human experience and religious ideas;
- engage and motivate students though active involvement in a range of activities;
- develop higher order thinking skills;
- promote greater understanding and acceptance of differing views and beliefs;
- develop skills of analysis, reasoning and discussion.

Links to the National Framework

The non-statutory National Framework for Religious Education has also guided the development of the material, particularly in that it:

- seeks to 'place value on the ethos and values that religious education can establish independent of any faith';
- states that RE should enable students 'to develop positive attitudes to their learning and to the beliefs';
- states that 'RE can transform students' assessment of themselves and others, and their understanding of the wider position of the world in which we live'.

The Framework states that RE should promote values of truth, justice, respect for all and care of the environment. There is also a special emphasis on:

- students valuing themselves and others;
- the role of family and community in religious belief and activity;
- the celebration of diversity in society through understanding similarities and differences;
- sustainable development of the Earth.

The **Beliefs and Issues** series supports the development of these values and attitudes through the subject matter covered and the learning activities that are suggested. Students are encouraged to listen to others, to express their own opinions openly and productively; to be able to disagree while maintaining respect for an opposing view and to be open to having their own opinions, beliefs and understanding challenged and possibly changed.

Using the series across Key Stage 3

The series of books are intended to be used across Key Stage 3. The National Framework for RE seeks to be 'robust' but also 'flexible'. The **Beliefs and Issues** material has also sought to balance these two facets. Although material is numbered, it is not necessarily intended to be used sequentially. Those responsible for overall planning need to have scope for creativity as they produce schemes of work for their individual situations. As a general rule, Year 7 students may concentrate on learning about religions and some of the explicit features of these, while certain moral and ethical issues may be better tackled in later years.

However, younger students should not be denied the opportunity to discuss issues with which they are confronted in other areas of life. For example, they will be aware of issues such as global poverty from television and other media coverage. They may well be actively engaged in addressing this, even if this is simply through buying and wearing a 'Make Poverty History' arm band. So, rather than dictating when a particular topic should be covered, the material is presented much more in discrete units which can be identified and allocated to particular points in the Key Stage programme by the teacher responsible.

The QCA Scheme of Work

The material relates to the QCA scheme of work but is not arranged to match it directly. For example, the QCA unit 7E is 'What are we doing to the environment?' In this QCA unit, students study the approaches of different religions to issues of conservation and stewardship, using a variety of sources to explore the teachings of different religions and how beliefs affect the lives of believers. They compare, contrast and evaluate the views of each religion and reflect on the relevance to their own lives of what they have learnt.

This unit can be covered through the **Beliefs and Issues** series with teachers locating and using the relevant sections from the Student Book and the Teacher Guide for each religion being studied by students in their school. It would be possible to revisit this topic at different stages, perhaps introducing ideas from different religions each time.

A similar approach can be used to tackle other QCA units, such as 9B 'Where did the universe come from?' or 9C 'Why do we suffer?', which require students to consider ideas from a number of different religious viewpoints as well as secular philosophies such as humanism.

There are close links with the 'knowledge, skills and understanding' and 'breadth of study' from the National Framework and these are made clear for each unit.

Using the Student Book and Teacher Guide
This book accompanies the *Muslim Beliefs and Issues* Student Book. It is intended to assist the teacher in making the most of that book by providing a flexible and useful resource which gives clear guidance for lessons based on the Student Book material.

The Teacher Guide has been written with both the non-specialist and the dedicated RE teacher in mind. The format for each piece is such that a non-specialist teacher has all that they require to deliver quality lessons which reflect the philosophical approach of the National Framework for RE. At the same time, the material is flexible enough for specialist teachers to use ideas from within the 'lessons' which can be incorporated into existing lessons or as part of the school's scheme of work.

The material is presented as discrete 'lessons', based on each double page spread of the Student Book. For each 'lesson', there is a starter activity, ideas for the main teaching section and a plenary and, in some cases, suggestions for the use of a photo from the CD-ROM as a stimulus for discussion. Relevant questions are provided for this activity which, like the starter activity, is intended to promote thinking skills.

- The starter activity is provided to stimulate the students' thoughts and encourage some interactivity. The starter is themed so that it can be used to lead directly into the rest of the session.
- The main teaching section gives instructions and guidance on how to work through the material in the Student Book. It contains suggestions for questions to stimulate discussion as well as background information where it is felt to be necessary. There are suggestions for additional activities which might be for individual students, pairs, small groups or the whole class.
- The plenary is included to indicate how best to draw a session to a close, recalling and reinforcing the main teaching points.
- Almost all the sessions have an associated Copymaster.
- A selection of 'display' files (in Word) have been provided for use on whiteboards or importing into PowerPoint, often indicated in the text by an emboldened 'display' or where text is highlighted on a whiteboard screen or on a scroll. These offer a visual stimulus for starter activities and reference materials for the main lessons and plenaries, and include the Copymaster files.

Although the above is the format for the presentation of the material, it is not the intention to limit the use of the material to individual lessons. It might be possible to work through a designated subject within that time frame but it may not give sufficient time for the students to really get to grips with some of the issues. There will be other reasons for wanting to spend more than one lesson on a given topic. Equally, there may be ideas from the books which you can use as part of an overall lesson you have planned around other material. In short, the material is presented as lessons and can be used as such but also contains 'stand alone' material which could be extracted for use outside the given format.

The activities in the Student Book are set out in the same order in the Teacher Guide. They are placed in the teacher guidance at the earliest point at which it would be sensible to ask the children to attempt them, usually when there has been some input or discussion. They provide for students to be actively engaged at points throughout the lesson. Beyond this, there is no strict timing for when the students carry out these tasks. So, for example, a teacher might feel that they would rather leave all the activities until the end of the direct teaching.

Additional activities and assessment
The activities offer an opportunity for a range of learning styles and provide a good deal of work for students. These are usually multi-ability tasks with differentiation being mainly by outcome. As has been said, the Teacher Guide also contains ideas for additional activities in the main teaching section. Neither these nor the Copymasters are intended as extension activities, available only to those who complete the exercises from the Student Book. They are activities which are intended to give further opportunities for students to reflect, analyse and respond and, in the case of the Copymasters particularly, to provide an assessment record indicating a student's level of understanding regarding a particular topic.

Some of the activities from the Student Book and the Teacher Guide would be suitable as homework projects, particularly some of the 'Take Time To Think' questions from the Student Book. Occasionally this suggestion is indicated in the material but, for the majority, this has been left to the discretion of the teacher or person responsible for RE planning.

Teacher Notes
WHAT IS ISLAM?

NATIONAL FRAMEWORK LINKS

1a: investigate and explain the differing impacts of religious beliefs and teachings on individuals, communities and societies

1c: investigate and explain why people belong to faith communities and explain the reasons for diversity in religion

1e: discuss and evaluate how religious beliefs and teachings inform answers to ultimate questions and ethical issues

2a: reflect on the relationship between beliefs, teachings and ultimate questions, communicating their own ideas and using reasoned arguments

3e: beliefs and concepts: the key ideas and questions of meaning in religions and beliefs, including issues related to God, truth, the world, human life and life after death

PHOTO STARTER

Display the photograph of the crescent moon. Ask students if they know which religion this symbol is associated with.

STARTER ACTIVITY

Display the words "Family", "Faith", "Obedience" and "Peace". Students copy these and write what they think each one means and how they experience these things in their own lives.

MAIN TEACHING

• Lead on from the starter by explaining that this activity illustrates central ideas in Islam. People who follow Islam say they are part of a family of believers, their faith is central to their lives, they seek to obey Allah (God) and to live in peace.

• Read through the introductory material and 'The Prophet Muhammad' with the students.

• Students complete 'Over To You' (1-5).

• Read through 'Islam in today's world' and identify the countries mentioned on the map. [See **display** file.]

• Ask students to suggest in which part of the world Islam began.
(present day Saudi Arabia)

• Ask what they think about the people in the countries mentioned who are not Muslims. Do they think they will have no religion or belong to another?
(This will vary according to the country. For example, the non-Muslim population in Egypt is mostly Coptic Christian. The aim is to highlight the fact that there are minority religions in Muslim countries.)

• Read through 'Islam and Muslims' with the students, recalling ideas from the starter.

• Students respond to the 'Take Time To Think' activity and complete Copymaster (1).

PLENARY

Use feedback from the Copymaster to discuss ideas about 'the attractions of this world' and about resisting the urge to do things that are not always 'for the best'.

1. Make a list of things you think of as temptations. You don't have to share anything really personal if you don't want to.

2. What temptations do you think people such as lottery winners or pop stars might have? Are they very different from yours? In what way?

3. What do you think Muslims might call 'the attractions of this life'? Would you agree?

4. How do Muslims seek to rise above these attractions?

5. Do you agree that there seems to be an element in most people's lives where they have to resist the desire to do certain things that are not always 'for the best'?

6. Where do these desires come from and why is it sometimes such a struggle?

WHO ARE THE MUSLIMS?

NATIONAL FRAMEWORK LINKS

1b: analyse and explain how religious beliefs and ideas are transmitted by people, texts and traditions

1c: investigate and explain why people belong to faith communities and explain the reasons for diversity in religion

2b: evaluate the challenges and tensions of belonging to a religion and the impact of religion in the contemporary world, expressing their own ideas

3e: beliefs and concepts: the key ideas and questions of meaning in religions and beliefs, including issues related to God, truth, the world, human life and life after death

PHOTO STARTER

Display the picture of the Muslims prostrating themselves. Ask students what they think the men are doing. Explain that this is part of praying. Ask why a person might assume this sort of position when they are praying. (In this case, it shows that the people are submitting to the will of Allah. People praying are recognising someone with greater authority.)

STARTER ACTIVITY

- **Display** the title "That's very kind".
- Give students five minutes to list all the ways that they could show kindness in a typical day. Prompt them with 'passive' ideas, such as 'I could not shout at my sister', and 'active' ideas, such as 'I could help make the packed lunches'.
- Discuss the importance of acts of kindness. What is the effect on other people when students are kind to them? How do the students feel when they receive kindness?

MAIN TEACHING

- Lead on from the starter by saying that showing kindness is a part of how we choose to live our lives. Explain that the lesson is about Muslim beliefs and how these affect their lives. Say that Islam is not simply about belief but is a way of life.
- Read through 'Their beliefs'. As you work through these, challenge the students to write a single sentence about each belief.
- Students complete 'Over To You' (1-2).

- Refer students to the text of 'A way of life' and the 'Check It Out' section. Consider each of the points in the 'Check It Out' section, asking students for examples of situations where these might be applicable:
  - *Take care of the poor.* Ask students to suggest where 'the poor' might be. Are these local people or would Muslims be concerned for poorer people wherever they may be? How might they respond to poverty locally and globally?
  - *Protect the weak.* Who do the students consider to be 'the weak' in our society today. What form can 'protection' take?
  - *Care for the aged.* What sort of care do elderly people need? Who do the students feel should be responsible for providing this care?
  - *Do good.* This is a very broad statement. What do the students take it to mean? Do we only 'do good' when we are responding to a 'bad' situation?
  - *Avoid evil.* What do students consider to be some of the 'evils' in the world? How can people, including Muslims, avoid these things?
  - *Be kind.* The students considered acts of kindness in the starter activity. Remind them of the 'passive' and 'active' distinction made in that activity.
- This discussion will assist students as they complete Copymaster (2) and 'Over To You' (3).
- Discuss the relationship between Islam, Christianity and Judaism before students consider the 'Take Time To Think' question. In unit 1, students learnt of some of the commonalities, such as the references to Ibrahim (Abraham), Musa (Moses) and Jesus. It is important to make clear that, although Muslims honour Jesus as a prophet, they do not believe he is the Son of God.
- Muslims recognise common origins in the Jewish scriptures (the Old Testament of the Bible), but they also believe that Jews and Christians have corrupted the original messages given by God by introducing certain errors and false teaching. The 'relationship' between Moses, Jesus and Muhammad for Muslims is that they are all prophets whose purpose is to bring God's word.

PLENARY

Students feed back their ideas from the Copymaster.

A WAY OF LIFE

Explain how a Muslim person might respond in these situations and how this behaviour reflects one of the things they strive to do in their life:

Remember that the Qur'an encourages every Muslim to:

- Do good
- Avoid evil
- Be kind
- Take care of the poor
- Protect the weak
- Care for the aged

3 Teacher Notes
SUNNI AND SHI'ITE MUSLIMS

NATIONAL FRAMEWORK LINKS
1b: analyse and explain how religious beliefs and ideas are transmitted by people, texts and traditions

1c: investigate and explain why people belong to faith communities and explain the reasons for diversity in religion

2b: evaluate the challenges and tensions of belonging to a religion and the impact of religion in the contemporary world, expressing their own ideas

3f: authority: different sources of authority and how they inform believers' lives

STARTER ACTIVITY

- **Display** the title "Who's in charge here?"
- Ask students to consider how a captain might be chosen for a sports team and what their role would be. What are the limitations on their role?
- In informal school situations, a captain might be chosen by popular consent. For a school team, a teacher or coach might appoint a captain. Captains are also appointed in professional circumstances.
- The students may identify qualities of skill, temperament, ability to lead, ability to encourage, the idea that they set a good example, etc.
- Point out that the limitations on the captain are the rules of the sport. These are laid down elsewhere.

MAIN TEACHING

- Introduce the topic, explaining that the Sunni and the Shi'ites are two groups within Islam.
- Read through the introductory material and 'The Sunni Muslims' with the students. Ask students to recall what the Qur'an is.
- Say that the Sunnah are the actions and practices of Muhammad. These were noted and recorded by those who knew him.
- Say that the Hadith is the collected sayings of Muhammad.
- Ask students to consider the starter activity. Explain that this is being used as an analogy. In the sports team scenario, ask students what they think the Qur'an, Sunnah and Hadith are represented by. *(the rules of the sport)*
- Read about leaders in Sunni communities. Ask about the sports team scenario and who is like the caliph. *(the team captain)*
- Ask students to identify the role of the caliph as given. *(to maintain law and order so that people could follow their religion and live in peace)*
- Ask about the role of a team captain. *(to ensure that team members follow the rules of the game and play well so that everyone enjoys playing their sport)*
- Say that the team captain does not make up the rules. The caliph does not do this either; he encourages people to obey them.
- Students complete 'Over To You' (1-2).
- Read through 'The Shi'ite Muslims' with the students. Referring to the sports team analogy, ask students how captains are chosen. *(they are usually 'elected' or appointed by a group of people)*
- Ask students to say what the Shi'ite Muslims believed about the new leader of the faith. *(that Muhammad had already appointed his cousin Ali as leader)* Point out that they were not disputing the central role of the Qur'an, the Sunnah or the Hadith.

- The Shi'ite community claim that Ali was the appointed successor to Muhammad and that he and all his descendents are the people who should lead the Islamic community and the Islamic states. The Sunni Muslims deny this, on the grounds that there is no written evidence to support the claim.
- Students refer to the 'Check It Out' section and complete 'Over To You' (3-5) using Copymaster (3).

PLENARY

Students recall the areas of agreement and difference between Shi'ite and Sunni Muslims.

Shi'ite Muslims	Sunni Muslims
1.	1.
2.	2.
3.	3.
4.	4.
5.	5.
6.	6.
7.	7.
8.	8.
9.	9.
10.	10.

Write the differences between these two groups in the respective spaces on the diagram below. Write what they agree on in the space where the two shapes overlap.

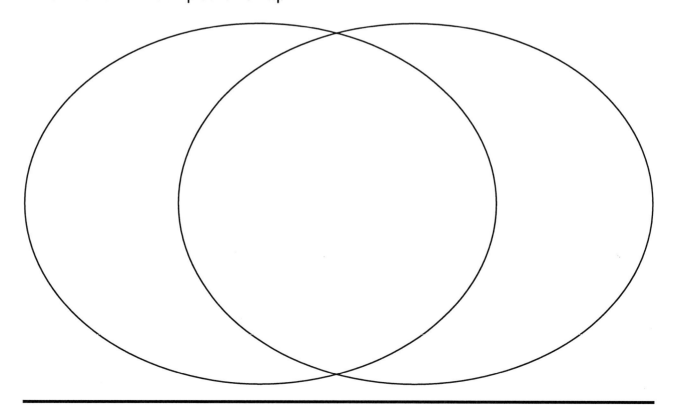

NATIONAL FRAMEWORK LINKS

1b: analyse and explain how religious beliefs and ideas are transmitted by people, texts and traditions

1d: analyse and compare the evidence and arguments used when considering issues of truth in religion and philosophy

1e: discuss and evaluate how religious beliefs and teachings inform answers to ultimate questions and ethical issues

2a: reflect on the relationship between beliefs, teachings and ultimate questions, communicating their own ideas and using reasoned arguments

3e: beliefs and concepts: the key ideas and questions of meaning in religions and beliefs, including issues related to God, truth, the world, human life and life after death

PHOTO STARTER

Display the picture of the notice above the mosque. Ask students to explain the significance of the notice. (Muslims believe in only One God, Allah. No other god should be recognised and certainly not worshipped. The mosque is a place to worship Allah.)

STARTER ACTIVITY

- **Display** these surnames and ask students to suggest what their origins might have been:

  Carter   Cooper   Fletcher   Naylor   Redman   Sawyer

  (A cart maker, a barrel maker, an arrow maker, a nail maker, a thatcher (from reed man) and a person who saws wood, respectively.)

- Write up some descriptive or inspirational first names, such as Daisy or Hope.
- Ask students if they know the origins and meaning of their names.

MAIN TEACHING

- Read through the introductory material and 'The names of Allah'. Explain that the names given are attributes of Allah, indicating subtleties and mysteries. These names are to help Muslims consider these different characteristics of Allah but, ultimately, it is impossible to know Allah fully because he is beyond our understanding.
- Talk about the tasbih beads. Ask students how they would assist a Muslim in their praying.
- Sometimes the beads are in strings of ninety-nine. These can be quite awkward or heavy and so beads are also prepared in strings of thirty-three. The beads in such a set are moved through three times. The beads are strung loosely so that they can be moved along easily. Each bead will be held lightly, usually between the thumb and forefinger, while one of the ninety-nine names is recited and the person thinks about what this name means for their own life and spiritual growth.
- Read through 'Allah is One' and 'Allah and the world', asking the students to identify what Muslims believe about Allah.

- Students complete 'Over To You' (1-4). *(There are a number of ideas associated with 'Over To You' (2). One is that there are, in fact, 100 names for Allah, since 100 is a perfect number and Allah is perfect. Only 99 names for Allah can be known because it is impossible to know all there is to know about him.)*
- Talk to the students about Islamic art. Figurative art is never found in a mosque or within the Qur'an. There are no pictures of Allah at all because he is pure spirit and so cannot be seen. To try to make an image of Allah would be offensive and idolatrous. There are no pictures or statues of Muhammad either. This is again because Muslims would be worried that people might be tempted to turn to idol worship. People should have their attention on Allah, not Muhammad. Muslims do express their beliefs through art, however. Sometimes this is through the beautiful calligraphy used for verses from the Qur'an, which are sometimes used as decorations in mosques. The Arabs who made up the early Muslim community were extremely interested in mathematics and worked with numbers, shapes and space. They felt that these things somehow reflected some of the beauties of the natural world and the universe. They used geometric designs to portray these ideas and show how Allah had created everything following careful designs.
- Students could research Islamic art and attempt to convey one of the names of Allah or part of his creation.
- Students complete Copymaster (4) (and 'Take Time To Think').

PLENARY
Students give feedback based on their ideas on the Copymaster (and 'Take Time To Think').

Decide which name of Allah a Muslim would concentrate on in these different situations. How might they feel when they have meditated on this name?

| If they had done something wrong | If they were worried about injustice |
| If they were worried about the future | If they were suffering |

Think of another of the 99 Names of Allah. Draw a situation where this characteristic would be particularly helpful for a Muslim to think about.

Teacher Notes

THE FIVE PILLARS OF ISLAM

NATIONAL FRAMEWORK LINKS

1a: investigate and explain the differing impacts of religious beliefs and teachings on individuals, communities and societies

1e: discuss and evaluate how religious beliefs and teachings inform answers to ultimate questions and ethical issues

2a: reflect on the relationship between beliefs, teachings and ultimate questions, communicating their own ideas and using reasoned arguments

3e: beliefs and concepts: the key ideas and questions of meaning in religions and beliefs, including issues related to God, truth, the world, human life and life after death

3f: authority: different sources of authority and how they inform believers' lives

STARTER ACTIVITY

- **Display** the following words or give out as sets of cards to groups. [Resource sheet (5)]

Having friends	*Being well off*	*Being part of a family*
Working hard	*Having a faith*	*Helping other people*
Abilities	*Clothes*	*Praying*

- Say that these are things some people say are the important things in their life. They are the foundations for some people and they help them live a happy and meaningful life.
- Students can individually list the items they agree with as making their life happy and meaningful.
- As a group, students could arrange the cards in a 'diamond nine' (one, two, three, two, one), with the most important at the top and the least important at the bottom.
- Students could record their 'diamond nine'.
- Students could then be asked to think how a religious (Muslim) person might arrange the cards. Are there any changes in the priorities?

MAIN TEACHING

- Introduce the topic, explaining that the work concerns the five things that are the foundations of the Islamic faith.
- Read through the introductory material and about the first two Pillars.
- Put students into groups to discuss the 'Take Time To Think' questions. Take feedback from the groups to identify the different things that give the students structure (for example, school terms and timetables, family routines, participation in regular clubs, activities, etc) and if and why they think structure is necessary.
- Students read about the remaining three Pillars and complete 'Over To You' (1-4).
- Responses to 'Over To You' (3) and (4) will provide starting points for the later sessions relevant to these topics.
- Students complete Copymaster (5).

PLENARY

Students talk about the Five Pillars, using their responses to 'Over To You'.

Having friends	Being well off	Being part of a family
Working Hard	Having a faith	Helping other people
Abilities	Clothes	Praying

In each of the boxes below, give the name of one of the Five Pillars of Islam. Briefly explain what each Pillar is and why it is important.

THE FAITH OF ISLAM

6 Teacher Notes
THE SHAHADAH

NATIONAL FRAMEWORK LINKS

1a: investigate and explain the differing impacts of religious beliefs and teachings on individuals, communities and societies

1b: analyse and explain how religious beliefs and ideas are transmitted by people, texts and traditions

2a: reflect on the relationship between beliefs, teachings and ultimate questions, communicating their own ideas and using reasoned arguments

3e: beliefs and concepts: the key ideas and questions of meaning in religions and beliefs, including issues related to God, truth, the world, human life and life after death

3h: expressions of spirituality: how and why human self-understanding and experiences are expressed in a variety of forms

PHOTO STARTER

Display the picture of the mu'adhin. Tell students that this person calls out five times a day from the mosque. Ask what they think he is calling people to. *(prayer)* Ask students about other features they can see in the photograph. The mu'adhin seems to be facing a particular feature. How would they describe this feature. *(an alcove)* Ask if anyone knows what this is called. *(mihrab)* Say that this is always positioned in a mosque facing the direction of a particular place. Ask students if they know what place this is. *(Makkah)* Discuss the clocks, asking what these might show *(times of prayer)*, and the seat, asking who might sit here *(the imam)* and why. If the imam sits here to deliver an address, the worshippers will see him clearly since they are seated on the floor.

STARTER ACTIVITY

- **Display** the title "That reminds me".
- If there is something students have to try to remember, how do they do this? *('Post-it' notes, messages on the fridge, writing on their hands, etc.)*
- Ask students to suggest things they need to be reminded about every day.
- Students discuss in pairs then feed back to class.

MAIN TEACHING

- Introduce the topic and remind students of the Shahadah as the most important of the Five Pillars of Islam.
- Read through 'The Shahadah' with the students, asking them to identify the Muslim belief that:
  - Allah is the one and only God.
  - Muhammad is the messenger / prophet of God.
- Read through 'The importance of the Shahadah' and 'The call of the mu'adhin'.
- Ask students to recall the benefit that Muslims receive from the regular five daily prayer times. *(It gives structure to their lives.)*
- Ask why Muslims will repeat the Shahadah to themselves many times during the day. *(They are keeping Allah, their faith and their duty at the forefront of their mind, always in their thoughts.)*

21

- Ask about the significance of whispering it to a new born baby and it being the last thing spoken before they die *(e.g. It is the most important thing in life from the beginning to the end. It marks the beginning and end of life.)*
- Students complete 'Over To You' (1-2).
- Can students find any flags for countries or organisations that have statements or mottos on them? Is there a school badge / motto? What do the mottos say / mean? How are these intended to make members of those countries / organisations feel?
- Tell the students that the Shahadah is written in Arabic on the flag of Saudi Arabia. Ask them why they think this is. What would it mean for citizens of that country?

PLENARY

Recall the main points of the lesson with questions and answers:

- Can anyone remember the Shahadah?

- What two main Muslim beliefs does it convey?

- On which two occasions is it especially important? *(birth and death)*

- What is the Shahadah used five times a day to do? *(call Muslims to prayer)*

7 Teacher Notes
SALAH

NATIONAL FRAMEWORK LINKS

1a: investigate and explain the differing impacts of religious beliefs and teachings on individuals, communities and societies

1b: analyse and explain how religious beliefs and ideas are transmitted by people, texts and traditions

1c: investigate and explain why people belong to faith communities and explain the reasons for diversity in religion

2b: evaluate the challenges and tensions of belonging to a religion and the impact of religion in the contemporary world, expressing their own ideas

3e: beliefs and concepts: the key ideas and questions of meaning in religions and beliefs, including issues related to God, truth, the world, human life and life after death

3h: expressions of spirituality: how and why human self-understanding and experiences are expressed in a variety of forms

PHOTO STARTER

Display the picture of the person washing. Ask students what the person is doing and why. Briefly discuss the idea of preparing to enter a sacred place or place of worship. Do the students think it is right to show respect when entering such a place? Is the washing only about removing physical dirt?

STARTER ACTIVITY

- **Display** the title "I never miss..."
- Students write down five things that they never fail to do during the week. Prompt them to think about watching particular television programmes, attending club meetings, music instrument practice, etc.
- Ask why these things are important or why they have to be done. Are the things on their lists all of their own choosing?
- Ask students to think about the things they are giving up in order to ensure they don't miss the things on their list.
- Is it sometimes difficult to meet a commitment to a particular activity?
- Students discuss their lists and other responses with a partner.

MAIN TEACHING

Commitment to prayer

- Thinking back to the starter activities, there may be some activities (e.g. practicing a musical instrument) that individuals could be distracted from and need discipline to persevere with. Ask for any students who can identify with this to describe their experiences.
- Introduce the topic of salah and read through the introductory paragraph. Discuss how this speaks of the distractions of the world and the need for discipline. Interrupting whatever is happening at these set times, either business or pleasure, reminds Muslims that Allah is more important than anything else.
- The five set times are dawn, noon, mid afternoon, sunset and nightfall.

Preparation for prayer

- Ask students about any times in which they take special care of their appearance. *(For example, when going out, attending a wedding or other function, or perhaps even when summoned by the head teacher!)*
- Ask why there is this preparation and the occasional need to 'look smart'. *(In most cases, a mark of respect in one way or another. Respect for the person or respect for the occasion.)*
- Read through 'Preparation for salah'
- Discuss the need for cleanliness in the mind (thoughts and feelings) and in the body. Ask students to say why this is. *(In prayer, Muslims are coming before Allah and need to be pure.)*
- Students can respond to the 'Take Time To Think' question.

What happens during salah?

- Read through 'Salah'. Talk about where salah takes place. *(It can take place anywhere that is clean.)*
- Ask why the place needs to be clean. *(purity / holiness of the activity)*
- Say that, although it can take place anywhere, it is felt to be preferable for Muslims to pray together. Ask why this would be. *(strengthens the feeling of community)*
- Discuss the set patterns of prayer. What are the benefits of these? *(Each movement expresses and accompanies different parts of the prayers. Joining in these movements together reinforces community. As these actions and words are used by Muslims around the world, they remind members of how they belong to the worldwide Muslim community.)*
- Tell the students about the importance of midday Friday Prayers. This is the most important time of prayer and worship. All adult men are expected to leave whatever they are doing in order to be present.
- Say that all prayer should be given with the person facing in the direction of Makkah.

  [www.islam.org has further information, illustrations and video]

The purpose of prayers

- Read through 'What is prayer about?' Put students into pairs, A and B.
- A must explain to B the first two points about prayer for Muslims. B then explains to A the second two.
- Students complete 'Over To You' (1-2) and Copymaster (7).

PLENARY

Students feed back their ideas from the Copymaster.

Additional information

Prayers

Fajr	Dawn Prayer	2 rak'ahs
Dhuhr	Midday Prayer	4 rak'ahs
Asr	Mid-afternoon Prayer	4 rak'ahs
Maghrib	Sunset Prayer	3 rak'ahs
'I'sha	An hour and a half later	4 rak'ahs

Rak'ah

1. When prayers begin, Muslims stand straight, hands by their side, facing the qiblah (direction of Makkah). They make a statement of intent.
2. They raise their hands to their ears and say "God is great."
3. Hands are moved down in front of the body, right over the left. A recitation from Surah 1 is given.
4. They bow from the hips, so the back is horizontal, and spread fingers over their knees. "Glory to my God the great!" is said three times.
5. Stand straight again, saying "God listens to those who thank him" and "Oh Lord, thanks be to you."
6. Worshippers then go onto their knees, with forehead and nose on the ground between their hands. In this position, "Glory to my Lord, the highest!" is said three times.
7. Sitting back on haunches, with hands on knees, they say "God is great."
8. There follows another prostration, as before, and "God is great!"
9. "Glory to my Lord the highest" is said again three times.
10. Standing up they say "God is great!"

The second rak'ah is done in the same way except that, following the first prostration, they sit upright and say "All prayer is for Allah... and worship and goodness."

Finally, still sitting, they look to the right and then to the left, saying "Peace be upon you and the mercy of Allah." This is addressed to those either side and to angels and departed spirits.

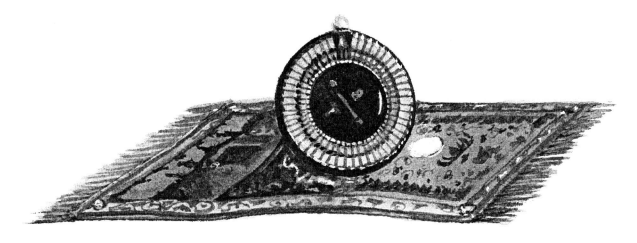

Look at this prayer mat.

It has a special feature which makes it especially useful for when a Muslim is travelling.

This is the . . . . This points towards . . . . ,

which is the direction Muslims must face to say prayers.

Muslims face this way because this was the birthplace of . . . .

Through the discipline of daily prayers, a Muslim is able to...

Through the discipline of . . . . , I am / would be able to...

Find out about the different positions of the rak'ah and what is recited.

DU'A

NATIONAL FRAMEWORK LINKS

1a: investigate and explain the differing impacts of religious beliefs and teachings on individuals, communities and societies

1b: analyse and explain how religious beliefs and ideas are transmitted by people, texts and traditions

1c: investigate and explain why people belong to faith communities and explain the reasons for diversity in religion

2b: evaluate the challenges and tensions of belonging to a religion and the impact of religion in the contemporary world, expressing their own ideas

3e: beliefs and concepts: the key ideas and questions of meaning in religions and beliefs, including issues related to God, truth, the world, human life and life after death

3h: expressions of spirituality: how and why human self-understanding and experiences are expressed in a variety of forms

PHOTO STARTER

Display the picture of the prayer beads. Ask students what they think this is. Explain that they are prayer beads. Ask students how they think prayer beads might be used. Say that the different beads help to remind the person praying about certain things. Sometimes they can be used to keep count of the number of times a particular phrase is repeated. Say that the students will find out about how Muslims use their prayer beads as they work through the unit.

STARTER ACTIVITY

- **Display** the title "Something on my mind".
- Ask students to be still and quiet. They should now focus on something that is concerning them. This could be something personal that they are happy to share, something to do with the school, local community or a national or international issue. Maintain silence and concentration on this issue for 1 minute.
- Put students into pairs to discuss their issues and what might be done.
- Ask individuals to give examples of their issues and possible actions.
- Say that these issues might prompt practical actions but, for members of a number of religious groups, they would also be the subject of prayer.

MAIN TEACHING

- Introduce the topic and read through the first page with the students. Ask students to identify the main differences between salah and du'a prayers. *(Salah are said at set times and using set words. Du'a can be said at any time and have no set words. Salah are said in Arabic; du'a can be spoken in the person's own language.)*
- Point out that du'a prayers would address the kind of issues from the starter activity.
- Students carry out 'Over To You' (1) and Copymaster (8). *(The Copymaster attempts to link particular thoughts with particular times of day. For example, a person might be more likely to think about the hungry of the world when they are about to enjoy their own lunch. This is not intended to suggest Muslims, or others, will always think about these things at these times.)*

- Read through 'Tasbih'. Ask students to consider the effect of repeating phrases such as "Glory be to Allah" after each bead of the tasbih. Ask them to recall some of the names of Allah (Unit 4). Point out that each bead represents one of the names of Allah. So, as each bead is passed through the fingers, a Muslim will recall one of these names and then say one of the phrases mentioned in the text. The combined result will be, for example, "The Compassionate. Thanks be to Allah"; "The All knowing. Allah is Great"; "The Everlasting. Glory be to Allah". Referring back to Unit 4, students could provide other combinations.
- Students complete 'Over To You' (2).
- Read through 'Bismillah' with the students. Ask them to give you details of the ceremony and explain its purpose. *(to mark the beginning of their religious education, reciting in Arabic and learning to pray)*

PLENARY
Students give feedback from the Copymaster.

PRAYERS FOR ALL OCCASIONS

Apart from their set prayers, Muslims can add in a du'a prayer during the formal prayers and also pray at other times. For each occasion, write what you think a Muslim might pray for and what you pray or think about on similar occasions.

First thing in the morning

A Muslim might pray about	I pray / think about

At midday

A Muslim might pray about	I pray / think about

At mid afternoon

A Muslim might pray about	I pray / think about

In the evening

A Muslim might pray about	I pray / think about

Last thing at night

A Muslim might pray about	I pray / think about

Before a long journey

A Muslim might pray about	I pray / think about

When something good has happened

A Muslim might pray about	I pray / think about

If someone I know is in trouble or worried

A Muslim might pray about	I pray / think about

9 Teacher Notes
THE HAJJ

NATIONAL FRAMEWORK LINKS
1b: analyse and explain how religious beliefs and ideas are transmitted by people, texts and traditions

1h: interpret a variety of forms of religious and spiritual expression

3e: beliefs and concepts: the key ideas and questions of meaning in religions and beliefs, including issues related to God, truth, the world, human life and life after death

3f: authority: different sources of authority and how they inform believers' lives

STARTER ACTIVITY

- **Display** the title "I've always wanted to go to..."
- Students work in pairs to describe places they have always wanted to visit and to say why.
- Take feedback from the pairs to create a list of reasons why people want to go to particular places.
- Students then discuss a place where they have been that is particularly special. This could be somewhere associated with visiting someone special or a major sporting or musical event. Students explain the feelings and emotions they had as they anticipated the trip, the journey there and how they felt during the visit.
- Take feedback to create a list of feelings and emotions associated with making a special journey.

MAIN TEACHING

- The starter activity aims to help the students understand that everybody has special places that they want to visit or have visited. It also suggests that there are many reasons why a place can be special to someone. In developing the lesson, draw out these parallels and the commonalities in feelings and emotions that might be experienced.
- Introduce the topic and explain that the Hajj is a very special journey for Muslims, which they go on to visit a place that is very special for them. Say that students will be thinking about why Muslims want to undertake this particular journey and about the emotions and feelings they experience.
- Read through the introductory paragraph. Students recall in which part of the world Makkah is located. (Refer to Student Book map, page 5 – see **display**.)
- Ask students questions to identify the main points:

> Who should undertake the Hajj? *(all healthy Muslims)*
>
> Who is excused? *(the old, sick, disabled and poor)*
>
> What is the destination of the pilgrims? *(Makkah and Medinah)*
>
> Why are these places special? *(birthplace of Muhammad, town where Muhammad settled and site of first mosque)*
>
> Why is joining with two million other pilgrims a 'blessing'?
>
> *(feel part of the Muslim family)*

- Say that the Hajj is one of the Five Pillars of Islam. Some of these Pillars are put into practise every day – they are a real part of everyday life for Muslims. The Hajj is the hardest of the Pillars to undertake for many and some are unfortunately unable to do it. Students read Extract A and complete 'Over To You' (1-2).
- Read about 'Ihram' and say that this is part of the preparation for Hajj.
- Ask students to consider why some of these things are required.
  (purity of mind and body)
- Say that the white clothing is also called ihram. Ask about the requirement for all men to wear the same white outfit. What else might this achieve apart from symbolising purity? *(It removes any outward signs of wealth or poverty that could be 'read' from a person's ordinary clothing. It helps pilgrims to feel that they are equal in the eyes of Allah – this is a crucial aspect of the Hajj.)*
- Read through 'The Hajj' and 'The Ka'bah'. You could show a short piece of video of part of the Hajj. [http://www.channel4.com/culture/microsites/H/hajj/ and http://news.bbc.co.uk/1/hi/world/middle_east/6212003.stm currently offer photos and clips]
- Students could undertake some further research to identify the significance of the Ka'bah and the 'Black Stone'. The Ka'bah houses the site where Ibrahim was commanded by Allah to build a shrine. The 'Black Stone' is housed in the south-east corner.
- Read 'After the Hajj' and ask students to consider how a Muslim might feel having completed the Hajj.
- Students complete Copymaster (9).
- Students could record the feelings they imagine a man or woman might have during the pilgrimage in the form of a diary page or postcard.
- Following the Hajj is the festival of Eid-ul-Adha. This festival is 'The festival of Sacrifice' and it commemorates Ibrahim's willingness to sacrifice his son to Allah. Allah provided a ram to be sacrificed in the boy's place. Each family should choose an animal for slaughter. The meat is shared, making sure that those who could not afford an animal of their own are also included in the sharing.

PLENARY
- Ask students to discuss some of the similarities and differences they have identified on the Copymaster.
- Although there are similarities with other 'special journeys', emphasise the fact that the Hajj is a deeply spiritual experience for Muslims, possibly the most significant of their lives.

Think of a special journey you have made or would like to make to a special place. List all the preparations you would make, how you would feel before and during the journey as well as when you arrive. Compare these to the preparations, feelings and emotions of a Muslim undertaking the Hajj.

My Special Journey	The Hajj
Destination	Destination
Why I want to go there	Why a Muslim wants to go there
Things I might take with me	Things a Muslim might take
Special clothes I might wear	Special clothes a Muslim might wear
Other preparations	Other preparations a Muslim will make
How I feel about going	How a Muslim might feel about going
What I like about the journey	What a Muslim might feel on the journey
What I will do when I am there	What a Muslim will do while there
How I might feel afterwards	How a Muslim might feel afterwards
What would you want to tell your friends about your experience?	What would a Muslim want to tell their friends about their experience?

10 Teacher Notes
THE DAY OF JUDGEMENT

NATIONAL FRAMEWORK LINKS

1a: investigate and explain the differing impacts of religious beliefs and teachings on individuals, communities and societies

1b: analyse and explain how religious beliefs and ideas are transmitted by people, texts and traditions

1d: analyse and compare the evidence and arguments used when considering issues of truth in religion and philosophy

1e: discuss and evaluate how religious beliefs and teachings inform answers to ultimate questions and ethical issues

2a: reflect on the relationship between beliefs, teachings and ultimate questions, communicating their own ideas and using reasoned arguments

3e: beliefs and concepts: the key ideas and questions of meaning in religions and beliefs, including issues related to God, truth, the world, human life and life after death

3o: discussing, questioning and evaluating important issues in religion and philosophy, including ultimate questions and ethical issues

3p: reflecting on and carefully evaluating their own beliefs and values and those of others in response to their learning in religious education, using reasoned, balanced arguments

STARTER ACTIVITY

- **Display** the title "Always on your best behaviour".
- Ask students to list occasions or situations in which particular standards or forms of behaviour are expected or required. *(For example, in libraries, restaurants, classrooms, in public places, etc.)*
- Ask students to consider the consequences of ignoring these expectations or the breaking of these 'rules'.
- Students can share their ideas in pairs and then feed back to the class.

MAIN TEACHING

- Develop the idea from the starter activity. The students are going to be considering the Muslim understanding of what happens when a person dies and the importance of living life according to particular guidelines. Say how we can understand something of the concept by thinking back to examples from the starter.
- Would students agree that there is a kind of unwritten rule that there are consequences to our behaviour?
- Ask students to provide examples of how certain behaviour is rewarded and certain behaviour is punished.
- Explain that, for Muslims, all behaviour and all actions throughout life lead to reward or punishment.
- Read through the introductory material and ask students to identify:
  - the help Muslims have in regard to making correct choices
  - the importance of correct motives
- Students can read through the remaining material and then complete 'Over To You' (1-3).
- Students could respond to the Muslim ideas of heaven and hell through poetry or painting / drawing.

- Students could suggest their own ideas about heaven and hell.
- Students complete Copymaster (10).

PLENARY
- Students bring feedback from the Copymaster.
- Recall the Muslim understanding of heaven and hell.

Read this quote from the atheist scientist and author Richard Dawkins:

> "I am trying to call attention to the elephant in the room that everybody is too polite – or too devout – to notice: religion, and specifically the devaluing effect that religion has on human life. I don't mean devaluing the life of others (though it can do that too), but devaluing one's own life. Religion teaches the dangerous nonsense that death is not the end."
>
> *Richard Dawkins*, Guardian, *Saturday Sept 15th 2001*

Dawkins is suggesting that a belief in life after death means that people value their physical life on this Earth less than they should and that they similarly give less value to the lives of other people. Do you agree with him? What evidence might a Muslim give to show that this is not the case?

If there is no judgement at the end of life, what would you say is the motivation for behaving in a particular way or for doing 'good deeds'?

11 Teacher Notes
THE UMMAH

STARTER ACTIVITY

- Ask students to consider people they have some responsibility towards. Explain that this could be directly, as in the case of having to look after younger brothers or sisters. Do they feel they have other responsibilities towards different members of their family? It could also be indirectly, as in a sense of responsibility for those who are less fortunate than them, such as victims of disasters or famine that they see on television and elsewhere.
- Do students feel a sense of responsibility towards other members of clubs or teams to which they belong? Do they have a sense of responsibility towards other people in school and is this only about their friends?
- Students discuss these ideas in pairs and feed back to the class.

MAIN TEACHING

- Introduce the topic and read through the opening paragraph. Say how the Ummah is a worldwide 'family' of believers. Explain that the students will be looking to see the ways in which Muslims show that they are part of this family.
- Work through 'The signs of Ummah' with the students, asking them to identify each sign as given:

> Friday prayers (noon)
> Set prayers and movements (rak'ahs)
> Facing Makkah during prayer
> Recitation of the Qur'an in Arabic
> The Hajj
> Charitable giving to poorer members

- Talk about the responsibilities the students identified in the starter activity. These ideas are often associated with belonging to a particular group. Put students into groups to discuss some of the benefits they feel from belonging to these groups (for example, mutual support, strength, encouragement, etc).

- Students complete Copymaster (11) and 'Over To You' (1-3).
- The Copymaster asks students to consider the groups they belong to, the responsibilities they have to those groups, how they take on those responsibilities and to show they care about the people in those groups and how they could strengthen any bonds that might exist.
- Surah 3:103 states:

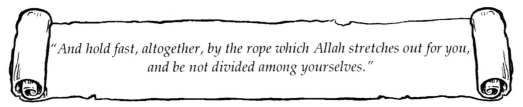

"*And hold fast, altogether, by the rope which Allah stretches out for you, and be not divided among yourselves.*"

Students could consider what the rope might be and how they visualise it.
- Students consider the 'Take Time To Think' question individually, then in pairs.

PLENARY

- Discuss the idea of corporate responsibility, as implied in the Copymaster.
- Ask students to recall the responsibilities a Muslim has towards other members of the Ummah and the benefits they receive from being part of it.

Think about each of the groups below. For each one, write down:
- the responsibilities you have
- how you meet those responsibilities
- how you show people in the group that you care
- how you can strengthen your relationships within the group

Family
Friends
School
Community
The world

Fill in the speech bubble to describe how a Muslim feels about belonging to the Ummah.

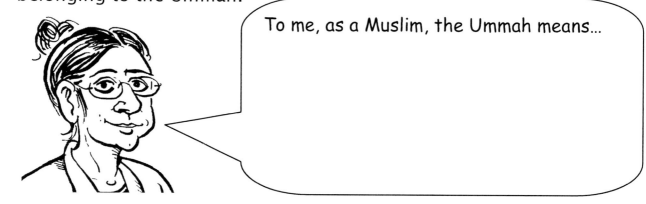

To me, as a Muslim, the Ummah means...

12 Teacher Notes
THE QUR'AN

NATIONAL FRAMEWORK LINKS

1a: investigate and explain the differing impacts of religious beliefs and teachings on individuals, communities and societies

1b: analyse and explain how religious beliefs and ideas are transmitted by people, texts and traditions

1g: interpret and evaluate a range of sources, texts and authorities, from a variety of contexts

2a: reflect on the relationship between beliefs, teachings and ultimate questions, communicating their own ideas and using reasoned arguments

3f: authority: different sources of authority and how they inform believers' lives

PHOTO STARTER

Display the picture of the adult reading the Qur'an. Ask students what they think the person is reading. Explain that this is the Holy Book of Islam. Ask students why they think it is important for a Muslim to read the Qur'an. *(They believe it is the revealed word of God. It contains guidance and instruction on how to live life properly.)*

STARTER ACTIVITY

- **Display** a car maintenance manual, a maths revision guide and a book of rules for a sport or game. If possible, show a copy of a law or Act of Parliament [http://www.opsi.gov.uk/acts/].
- Ask students in pairs to identify:
  - the people for whom each book is relevant.
    (an owner of the particular model of car, a person studying for a maths exam, people who want to play that sport, citizens of the country to which the law relates)
  - the authority that each of these publications has.
    (they are all authoritative and therefore trustworthy)
  - the content and 'use' of each.
    (a mixture of advice, information, instructions and rules)
- Use feedback from the pairs to discuss the range of publications. Talk about how the maths revision guide might only be relevant to those who are taking the exam but the 'maths' is the same for everyone.
- Talk about how the law of the land applies to everyone but might only be directly relevant to a person if, for example, they set up a business (Company Law) or are the victim of a crime.

MAIN TEACHING

- **Display** a picture or a copy of the Qur'an and ask students if they can identify it.
- Read through the introductory paragraph in the Student Book.
- Recap the story of the 'Night of Power' with the students.

Additional information.

Muhammad spent a long time praying each day in a cave on Mount Hira. He was concerned about the way of life of the people living around him. They were drinking too much, gambling and mistreating their wives and others less fortunate than themselves. One day in the cave, Muhammad had a vision of the Angel Jibril. The angel told him to read aloud from a text in front of him. Jibril told Muhammad that he would be a messenger from God. The messages continued for several months and they form the basis of what is written in the Qur'an.

- Explain that Muslims believe the Qur'an to be received directly from God. It has not been altered or corrupted in any way. It can only be properly understood and recited in Arabic. Translations of the Qur'an are permitted but are not considered to be the same. They are regarded as useful for study by non-Arabic speakers and are referred to as 'interpretations' rather than translations. This is because the language and the content together create a whole which is not truly available if either one is missing.
- Students read through the material in 'The Qur'an' and complete 'Over To You' (1-3).
- Remind students of the meaning of the word 'Islam' (to submit) and that Muslims submit themselves to the will of Allah.
- The Qur'an gives guidance on how to live a life that pleases Allah rather than simply giving rules.
- Students read through 'The teachings of the Qur'an' and complete Copymaster (12).
- Students respond to the 'Take Time To Think' question.

PLENARY

Ask for examples of situations where individuals might need guidance.

Write down some of the guidance Muslims receive from the Qur'an in regard to how they should live.

Write down some guidance you think would be helpful for people seeking to live a good life which will bring them and others happiness.

13 Teacher Notes
USING THE QUR'AN

NATIONAL FRAMEWORK LINKS

1a: investigate and explain the differing impacts of religious beliefs and teachings on individuals, communities and societies

1b: analyse and explain how religious beliefs and ideas are transmitted by people, texts and traditions

1g: interpret and evaluate a range of sources, texts and authorities, from a variety of contexts

2a: reflect on the relationship between beliefs, teachings and ultimate questions, communicating their own ideas and using reasoned arguments

3f: authority: different sources of authority and how they inform believers' lives

3h: expressions of spirituality: how and why human self-understanding and experiences are expressed in a variety of forms

PHOTO STARTER

Display the picture of the child reading the Qur'an. Ask the students what is significant about the picture. *(It is a child reading.)* Ask what the significance of this is. *(That children are taught from an early age to read the Holy Book of Islam.)*

STARTER ACTIVITY

- **Display** the title "I know it off by heart".
- Ask students to write down a piece of poetry, drama, novel or song lyric that they know 'off by heart'. Students could recite one or two examples.
- Talk about the phrase 'off by heart' and say that its origins are obscure, but that the heart was felt to be the seat of feelings, thoughts, etc. Therefore, if something was learnt really well, it could be said to be taken into the heart.
- Talk about the significance of learning something by heart. *(You no longer need the source material with you. It becomes a part of you and is available at any time.)*

MAIN TEACHING

- Read through the introductory material and 'Muslim schools' with the students.
- Students complete 'Over To You' (1-2).
- Discuss students' responses to 'Over To You' (1-2). Ask students:

  - What might it mean for a young Muslim to 'learn about their faith'?
  - What aspects of the faith will be covered in terms of beliefs, teachings and ideas?
  - How might these things influence the way a person tries to live their life?
  - Why would Muslims need to learn Arabic?
    (This leads on to the next section.)

- Read about 'Learning the Qur'an'. Remind students of the fact that translations of the Qur'an are sometimes referred to as interpretations, since Muslims believe that it cannot be translated into another language and retain its beauty and true meaning.

- Say that many Muslims learn to recite the Qur'an in Arabic, even if it is not their first language. They gain their understanding from 'interpretations' or from an imam.
- Students can consider the 'Take Time To Think' question.
- Read through 'Friday Prayers' with the students.
- Talk about the role of the imam. Explain that he is not like a rabbi in Judaism or a member of the ordained clergy in certain Christian Churches. The imam may be seen as a guardian of the mosque. He is not regarded as being a 'holy' man, set apart from others, although he will lead prayers and, for some, be their spiritual leader.
- Students complete 'Over To You' (3) and Copymaster (13).

PLENARY

Students give feedback from the Copymaster regarding what they think Muslims might learn from the different verses of the Qur'an.

Possible responses to the Copymaster verses	
11:116	Be contented with what you have, do not be jealous of other people's wealth.
7:111	God is one, there is only one God (specifically God is not a Trinity as in the Christian understanding).
83:1-3	People who are dishonest in business will be punished on the Day of Judgement.
2:44	You should behave towards other people the way you expect them to behave towards you.
35:1	Allah created the world and everything in it. He controls everything.
17:31	It is wrong to take life – only Allah can decide when a person should die. Allah will provide for people in difficult circumstances.
5:90	Certain things are forbidden to Muslims: alcohol (and other intoxicants), gambling (because it can lead to poverty), worshipping idols (because there is no God but Allah), divination (which is associated with the occult or false spirits).

13 Copymaster
WHAT DO MUSLIMS LEARN FROM THE QUR'AN?

Read these verses from the Qur'an and write what you think they teach Muslims about their beliefs and their actions:

Verses from the Qur'an	What a Muslim could learn from the verses
Don't desire that which Allah has bestowed on some of you and not others. (11:116)	
Say 'Praise be to Allah, who begets no son and who has no partner in his kingdom.' (7:111)	
Cheaters will suffer terribly. They insist on full measure when they have people measure something for them, but when they have to *give* by weight or measure they give less than is due. (83:1-3)	
Why do you ask of others proper conduct and you yourselves forget it? (2:44)	
Praise be to Allah, who created the heavens and the earth, who made the angels, messengers with wings two, or three or four. He adds to creation as he pleases: for Allah has power over all things. (35:1)	
Do not kill your children in fear of poverty, we shall provide for both them and you. Killing them is a big sin. (17:31)	
O you who believe! Alcohol and gambling , idols and divining by using arrows are only a filthy work of Satan; give them up so you may do well. (5:90)	

Teacher Notes
THE SUNNAH

NATIONAL FRAMEWORK LINKS

1a: investigate and explain the differing impacts of religious beliefs and teachings on individuals, communities and societies

1b: analyse and explain how religious beliefs and ideas are transmitted by people, texts and traditions

1g: interpret and evaluate a range of sources, texts and authorities, from a variety of contexts

2a: reflect on the relationship between beliefs, teachings and ultimate questions, communicating their own ideas and using reasoned arguments

3f: authority: different sources of authority and how they inform believers' lives

STARTER ACTIVITY

- **Display** the title "Leading by example".
- Ask students to provide a definition for this phrase and to think of one or two examples of how it could be put into practice.
- They could think of individuals who, in their opinion, lead by example or whose example they try to follow.
- Students could discuss their ideas in pairs then feed back to the class.

MAIN TEACHING

- Draw out the point from the starter about leading by, and learning from, example. Contrast this with people who have perhaps only written a book of instructions or say things they do not necessarily put into practice themselves. Ask students whether they think they would be more likely to follow someone who puts what they say into practice.
- Introduce the topic and read through 'The Hadith' with the students.
- Ask students to explain what the Hadith contains and why they are valuable. *(They are sayings of Muhammad and his close companions which expand and illustrate verses from the Qur'an, which are easier to understand and cover all aspects of life.)* Say that these sayings were handed down originally by word of mouth before being collected and written down.
- Students complete 'Over To You' (1-2).
- Read through 'The Sirah' and discuss them with reference to biographies written today.
- Ask students to explain the difference between a biography and an autobiography and the difference between an authorised biography and an unauthorised biography. Explain that there were many 'biographies' of Muhammad written which were not always accurate and did not contain information which could be trusted. *(Not all were like authorised biographies.)* A system was developed to decide whether a tradition contained in the Sirah was authentic.
- Ask the students why it is important for these things to be verified. *(Muslims are using the sayings and accounts of the life of Muhammad as an example, referring back to the starter activity.)*

- Say that, for Muslims, the Qur'an is the book that has the most authority, followed by the Hadith and the Sirah. Ask students why they think the writings are in this order. *(The Qur'an contains the words of Allah and is his eternal record. The Hadith are the words of men (Muhammad and his companions) and are therefore open to discussion. The Sirah, similarly, concern a man.)*
- Read 'The Sunnah' and make sure students understand what this is. *(The name given to the sayings of Muhammad [Hadith] and the life of Muhammad [Sirah].)* Explain that the word 'Sunnah' means 'practice' in the sense of a habit or custom. *(For example, 'It was his practice to...')* The Sunnah applies particularly to those things Muhammad did as a prophet.
- Students complete 'Over To You' (3).

PLENARY

Students present their ideas from 'Over To You' (2).

NATIONAL FRAMEWORK LINKS

1a: investigate and explain the differing impacts of religious beliefs and teachings on individuals, communities and societies

1b: analyse and explain how religious beliefs and ideas are transmitted by people, texts and traditions

2b: evaluate the challenges and tensions of belonging to a religion and the impact of religion in the contemporary world, expressing their own ideas

3h: expressions of spirituality: how and why human self-understanding and experiences are expressed in a variety of forms

3i: ethics and relationships: questions and influences that inform ethical and moral choices, including forgiveness and issues of good and evil

STARTER ACTIVITY

- **Display** the title "Happy Families".
- Ask students to suggest things that go towards making a happy family. What would it be like in an ideal family? Do they think that it would be best if children could make up their own minds about everything and make all their own decisions? *(Is the family a place to learn about life, to make mistakes in safety, to be corrected, to be guided in decision-making, etc?)*

MAIN TEACHING

- Using the material in the Student Book, model the beginning of a web diagram with 'A Muslim Family' as the centre. From this centre, begin to draw out 'arms' dealing with different aspects of the family [see **display**]:

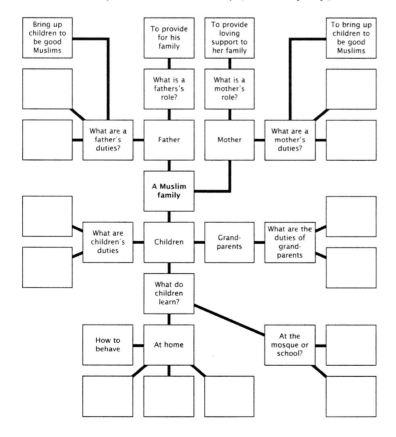

- Model as much of this as you think is necessary before telling students that they should copy and complete it, using information from the Student Book. (From these suggested 'question boxes', the students go on to add the 'answer boxes', expanding the diagram as they do so.) Resource sheet (15) contains a blank template of the diagram, if required.
- Students complete 'Over To You' (1-3) and answer the 'Take Time To Think' questions.
- Students complete Copymaster (15).

PLENARY

Use student feedback from the Copymaster and exercises to recap the main teaching points about Muslim family life.

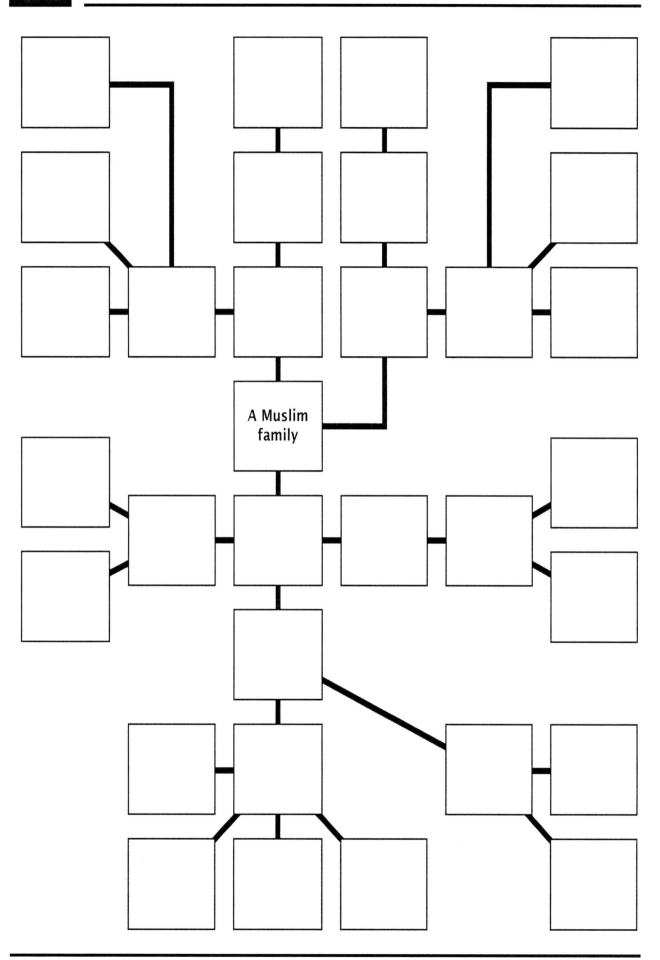

A Muslim family

Look at these pictures and say what you think is happening.

What benefits do you think Muslim children gain from being in a family? Put your ideas in groups, using these headed columns:

Practical	Emotional	Spiritual

Why do you think Muslims are taught that they should take care of orphans?

NATIONAL FRAMEWORK LINKS

1a: investigate and explain the differing impacts of religious beliefs and teachings on individuals, communities and societies

1b: analyse and explain how religious beliefs and ideas are transmitted by people, texts and traditions

2b: evaluate the challenges and tensions of belonging to a religion and the impact of religion in the contemporary world, expressing their own ideas

3h: expressions of spirituality: how and why human self-understanding and experiences are expressed in a variety of forms

3i: ethics and relationships: questions and influences that inform ethical and moral choices, including forgiveness and issues of good and evil

STARTER ACTIVITY

- What events happen in childhood to mark special occasions?
- Students recall special times from their past, such as celebrations or holidays they remember. What makes these events memorable?
- Students discuss their ideas in pairs before feeding back to the class.

MAIN TEACHING

- Develop the idea of special occasions from the starter. Most students will probably cite regular celebrations to mark their birthdays as important childhood events.
- Ask why birthday parties occur. *(They are marking a special event – the birth of a child.)*
- Say that, in many cultures and traditions, there are three major events in childhood which are often marked by special ceremonies: Birth, Naming, Initiation (**display** these headings).
- Either: deal with each in turn, explaining why each is significant and compare with the examples from the Muslim faith, or deal with all three and then consider the Muslim examples. *(Material below reflects this format.)*

Birth

The birth of a baby is always a significant event. In traditional cultures, when this happens within a family and community, its importance is increased because it signifies a continuation of a family line and of the existence of the community. It is a happy event and a cause for celebration in a family.

Naming

In many cultures, the naming of a child is very significant. A child's name may be used to indicate a family line. It might be given in the hope of imparting some desirable characteristics onto the child, such as bravery, integrity or happiness.

Initiation

Again, many cultures and traditions have ceremonies which are seen to mark the end of 'childhood'. After this point, in many senses, the young person is treated as an adult member of the community to which they belong.

- Students can discuss any of these that they are aware of in their own backgrounds.
- Introduce the topic of Muslim childhood by saying that the students will be considering how events in childhood are marked by members of that faith.
- Read through the introductory material and 'Birth' from the Student Book. Ask students to identify:
  - how a new child is viewed *(as a gift from Allah)*
  - what they become part of *(the Ummah)*
  - the significance of the adhan being spoken into the child's ear *(the first words it hears are about Allah)*
- Students read through 'The aqiqah ceremony' and complete 'Over To You' (1) and 'Take Time To Think'. *(The sacrifice is a way of giving thanks to Allah for the blessing of the child, and the sharing of the meat with the poorer members of the community includes them in this thanksgiving.)*
- Read through 'The bismillah ceremony' with the students. Say that this is not an initiation ceremony but rather the beginning of a process which could be viewed as a long initiation. This marks the beginning of a child's education in the way of their faith. There is no particular initiation ceremony in Islam. Rather, a child is deemed to be an 'adult' in the faith when they can partake of all the necessary religious observances.
- Students complete 'Over To You' (2).
- Read through the material about 'Khitan'. Explain that there is no reference to circumcision in the Qur'an but that it is accepted since it is mentioned in the tradition (Hadith) and books of Islamic law. The practise is not unique to Islam and the custom pre-dates this religion in the part of the world where it began.
- Ask students what they think the significance of circumcision might be. *(a physical sign of commitment to a faith)* It is regarded as a religious duty for those who would profess Islam.

PLENARY
Ask students to recall the ceremonies that mark out childhood for Muslims.

17 Teacher Notes
MARRIAGE

NATIONAL FRAMEWORK LINKS

1a: investigate and explain the differing impacts of religious beliefs and teachings on individuals, communities and societies

1b: analyse and explain how religious beliefs and ideas are transmitted by people, texts and traditions

1e: discuss and evaluate how religious beliefs and teachings inform answers to ultimate questions and ethical issues

1h: interpret a variety of forms of religious and spiritual expression

2b: evaluate the challenges and tensions of belonging to a religion and the impact of religion in the contemporary world, expressing their own ideas

3h: expressions of spirituality: how and why human self-understanding and experiences are expressed in a variety of forms

3i: ethics and relationships: questions and influences that inform ethical and moral choices, including forgiveness and issues of good and evil

3p: reflecting on and carefully evaluating their own beliefs and values and those of others in response to their learning in religious education, using reasoned, balanced arguments

STARTER ACTIVITY

- **Display** the question "What's the point of marriage?"
- Students consider the statements on Resource Sheet (17) and put them in a line from 'strongly agree' to 'strongly disagree'.
- Students compare and discuss their arrangements in pairs or small groups before feeding back to the class.

MAIN TEACHING

- Introduce the topic and develop the lesson by saying that students will consider some Muslim views on marriage.

Additional information

For Muslims, the basic unit of society is the family and the foundation of a family is marriage. Marriage is the only context in which sexual activity is permitted and is recommended, in part, as a means of avoiding all unlawful sexual practices.

Customs related to marriage vary widely across the cultures which the participants represent. The central ideas of the presence of witnesses and the existence of a marriage contract are always essential.

Although the marriage is a civil rather than a religious ceremony, there are elements of a festive occasion. For example, the bride may wear elaborately decorated clothes and shawls. In some cultures, her hands are decorated with intricate patterns. The groom may wear a colourful wedding garland. There is often a procession and a wedding party in celebration of the occasion.

- Read through the introductory paragraph and 'What does the Qur'an expect?' Ask students to identify the qualities a husband and wife are expected to show from this verse. *(love and kindness)*

- Students complete 'Over To You' (1), which asks for the reason for marriage. *(that men and women might live in peace with one another)*
- Read through 'Arranged marriages' and look at the 'Take Time To Think' question. Let students discuss the issues concerning arranged marriages. Do they think they should be able to choose who they marry?
- Explain that marriage in Islam is not just about the two people getting married. It is much more the joining of two families.
- Students complete 'Over To You' (2).
- Read through 'More than one wife?' and ask students how they would feel about this.
- Say that a Muslim man should only take more than one wife if he can care for them adequately.
- Read through 'The marriage contract and ceremony' and 'Check It Out'.
- Students complete 'Over To You' (3-5) and Copymaster (17). *(Muslim students can complete part two of the Copymaster by suggesting some other, secular, ideas about marriage.)*
- A further activity could be to arrange the statements from the starter activity in the way in which a Muslim might place them in terms of agreeing and disagreeing.

PLENARY

Use questions and answers to recall the main points about Muslim marriage:

- Where can a Muslim marriage take place? *(at home or in a mosque)*
- Who has to be at the wedding? *(at least two witnesses)*
- What does 'an arranged marriage' mean?
  (people other than the bride and groom choose their partners)
- What does the groom's family give to the bride's family?
  (a payment or 'dowry')
- What is the purpose of marriage in regard to society?
  (it is the foundation for the family which is the basic unit of society)
- What happens after the wedding ceremony?
  (there is a procession and a party)

Marriage is the best way of two people showing they love each other.	Marriage lets people show that they are committed to each other.
If people really love each other, there is no need for them to get married.	Marriage is the best basis for family life.
Marriage and family keep a society together.	A person should only marry someone they really love.
Only married people should have sexual relations because they are really committed to each other.	Married couples should support one another in everything they do.

DIFFERENT VIEWS ON MARRIAGE

Write what you think these young Muslim people might say about marriage.

Write what you think about marriage.

18 Teacher Notes
DEALING WITH DEATH

STARTER ACTIVITY

- **Display** the title "Fondly remembered".
- Tell students that people often have a simple inscription made on the headstone of a grave. This is called an epitaph and is usually text which honours the deceased person. Ask students to consider how they would like to be remembered. What about themselves would they like people to be honouring?
- Students discuss their ideas in groups and feed back to the class.
- Talk about how an epitaph recognises how a person has behaved during their lifetime.

MAIN TEACHING

- Introduce the topic and read through the material about 'The example of Muhammad'. Ask students to say what this teaches about Muslim beliefs about life after death and how they seek to approach death. *(They believe they will go to Paradise if they have lived a good life and so try to approach death calmly.)*
- Students complete 'Over To You' (1).
- Read through the first part of 'Before and after death' with the students. Ask them to recall the Shahadah and to say what this is. (*"There is no God but Allah. Muhammad is the messenger of Allah."* *This is a declaration and affirmation of faith.*)
- Ask why it would be significant to say the Shahadah as a person approaches death.
- Ask why a person might ask for forgiveness of sins from those around. (*It is recognition that sins may have been committed and a chance to have them forgiven. If the forgiveness is received, the dying person will be more peaceful.*)
- Ask what sort of passages might be read. (For example, those that speak of Allah's forgiveness and the promises of life after death.)
- Ask what sort of prayers might be said. (For example, prayers for a release of pain, or for Allah to be merciful to the dying person.)
- Students complete 'Over To You' (2).
- Ask students to read about what happens after death and to complete 'Over To You' (3).
- Read the first paragraph from 'The visit of two angels', which mentions mourning. Put students into pairs or small groups to discuss why people are still sad when someone dies, even if they believe that there is a 'life after death'. Take feedback.
- Talk about the need to express feelings associated with the death of someone close.

- Say that grief at the death of someone close is a universal human response.
- Students might be willing to share in their pairs about any experiences they have had of death. You will need to be sensitive if any students have had a recent bereavement.
- Read through the remainder of the material about angels. Muslims are well aware of the promises of Paradise and of the torments of hell from the Qur'an and from descriptions from later traditions. However, Muslims are also encouraged to view living a good life as a matter of accountability and responsibility to Allah, rather than because of any promise of Paradise or threat of hell.
- Students complete 'Over To You' (4) and consider the 'Take Time To Think' question.
- Students complete Copymaster (18). If you have Muslim students, they can answer 3) and 4) by suggesting how they think a humanist or atheist might answer.

PLENARY

Students feed back their ideas from the Copymaster.

In the first Surah of the Qur'an, Muslims ask Allah to guide them in the right path, the path of those who will receive his blessing, not the path of those who have angered him or who have gone astray. This is the hope they have when they are facing death; that they have stayed on this 'right path'.

1) What do you think Muslims try to do in their lives to show that they are on the 'right path'?

2) What do you think a Muslim would consider behaviour which would anger Allah or be seen as 'going astray'?

3) Which of the actions in 1) would you say are 'good' and worth using as an example for your own life? Which do you disagree with and why?

4) Which of the actions in 2) would you agree with as 'wrong' or as signs that someone is not leading the kind of life they should? Which do you disagree with and why?

19 Teacher Notes
THE PLACE OF WOMEN IN ISLAM

NATIONAL FRAMEWORK LINKS

1a: investigate and explain the differing impacts of religious beliefs and teachings on individuals, communities and societies

1b: analyse and explain how religious beliefs and ideas are transmitted by people, texts and traditions

1c: investigate and explain why people belong to faith communities and explain the reasons for diversity in religion

2b: evaluate the challenges and tensions of belonging to a religion and the impact of religion in the contemporary world, expressing their own ideas

2e: express their own beliefs and ideas, using a variety of forms of expression

3i: ethics and relationships: questions and influences that inform ethical and moral choices, including forgiveness and issues of good and evil

3j: rights and responsibilities: what religions and beliefs say about human rights and responsibilities, social justice and citizenship

STARTER ACTIVITY

- **Display** the title "A woman's place".
- Ask students to consider the phrase "A woman's place is in the home."
- Do they agree at all with the idea that women:
  - are better at bringing up children?
  - are better at running a home?
- Students discuss in pairs then feed back to the class. Record ideas for reference.

MAIN TEACHING

- Talk about how the role of people in society is always changing. Historical or traditional roles sometimes become unworkable as a society changes.
- Discuss the role of women and men in recent times in the UK. Talk about how these roles have changed. Huge changes occurred during the 20th century. Many women experienced work in traditionally 'male' roles during and after the First World War. The arrival of offices and, with them, secretarial positions meant that many more jobs for women became available. Prior to this, they had been more restricted to home-working, laundry and domestic service work.
- Talk about the effect of culture on gender roles. In the UK, medicine has traditionally been male-dominated and so most doctors are men. In Russia, where medicine has been seen as a much more female-oriented role, most doctors are women. Conversely, in the UK we have special terms such as 'male nurse' to alert us to the fact that men are increasingly taking up this role, which was almost exclusively female.
- The discussion will give a context to the place of women in Islam. This 'place' is seen differently by Muslims in different parts of the world and with different views on interpreting Islamic teaching.
- Read through the introductory material and 'Women in Islam'.
- Underline the fact that Islam views men and women as equal in terms of faith and education. The differences are in roles and duties.
- Read through 'Check It Out' (1) and help students to identify the duties of women: family, domestic and religious.
- Read through 'Check It Out' (2) and identify men's duties: provider, family and religious.

- Students complete 'Over To You' (1-3).
- Read through 'The modern roles of women in Islam'.
- The first paragraph discusses employment and careers. Many Muslims believe that women can work, as long her duties to the home and family are met. The Qur'an mentions women earning money (4:32).
- The second paragraph deals with men and women praying together in public. Again, Muslim opinion varies. Some feel that this is acceptable and many mosques have a separate place for women to pray. Others feel that it is better for a woman to observe prayers at home. The teaching of the Qur'an means that, theoretically, women are permitted to become learned in Islam and even to become scholars. They are not, however, permitted to lead prayer for men or mixed groups but may do so for a group of other women.
- The third paragraph considers how some of these viewpoints are combined by Muslims in the UK.
- Students complete 'Over To You' (4) and Copymaster (19).

PLENARY

Students give feedback from the Copymaster to identify the different views of Muslims on the role of women and any personal views they have.

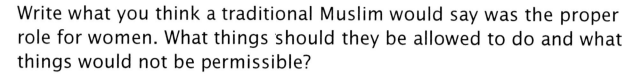

Write what you think a traditional Muslim would say was the proper role for women. What things should they be allowed to do and what things would not be permissible?

Write what you think a more liberal, modern Muslim might say about the role of women. What would they be expected to do and what might not be allowed?

What do you think the 'role of women' is? Do women have any special roles or responsibilities? Is there anything that a woman should not be allowed to do?

NATIONAL FRAMEWORK LINKS

1a: investigate and explain the differing impacts of religious beliefs and teachings on individuals, communities and societies

1b: analyse and explain how religious beliefs and ideas are transmitted by people, texts and traditions

1e: discuss and evaluate how religious beliefs and teachings inform answers to ultimate questions and ethical issues

2b: evaluate the challenges and tensions of belonging to a religion and the impact of religion in the contemporary world, expressing their own ideas

3i: ethics and relationships: questions and influences that inform ethical and moral choices, including forgiveness and issues of good and evil

3j: rights and responsibilities: what religions and beliefs say about human rights and responsibilities, social justice and citizenship

STARTER ACTIVITY

- **Display** the question "Who's in the family?"
- Ask students to write down the people they consider to be members of their family. How far does the family 'spread'? (*parents, grandparents, uncles, aunts, nephews, nieces, cousins, etc*)
- How often do they see the different family members?
- Students can share their responses with a partner then feed back to the class. Record the different responses for reference.

MAIN TEACHING

- Introduce the topic and read through the first paragraph. Discuss the difference between a Muslim position on looking after the elderly and the options available in today's society in the UK. (*Warden assisted accommodation, nursing homes, etc.*)
- Read through 'The extended family'. Refer to the starting activity and compare. Does anyone live in an 'extended family' situation? Do students have a close knit larger family group that live close together if not in the same dwelling?
- Students respond to the 'Take Time To Think' question and 'Over To You' (1-2).
- Students could discuss their own grandparents and the relationships they have.
- Students read through 'Grandparents' and the 'Check It Out' section and complete 'Over To You' (3-6).
- Work through and discuss students' responses to 'Over To You' (3-6). Note that 'Over To You' (5) can refer to both young children and 'adult' children. The first are mentioned as being taught to show respect to parents and grandparents. As adults, people are still 'children' of their parents. They must show them respect and also be ready to provide practical care and support.
- Students respond to Copymaster (20).

PLENARY

- Students bring ideas from the Copymaster and the 'Take Time To Think' question to the class.
- Students respond to 'Over To You' (7) or take this as a homework assignment.

Some people in old age feel that they are a burden and do not have much to offer. Do you think this is true? What could elderly people have to offer? Is a person only valuable for as long as they can work and make an active contribution to a society?

What help can older members of a family offer to younger members?

Why do you think Muslims seek to treat their elderly members with care and respect?

NATIONAL FRAMEWORK LINKS

1a: investigate and explain the differing impacts of religious beliefs and teachings on individuals, communities and societies

1b: analyse and explain how religious beliefs and ideas are transmitted by people, texts and traditions

1c: investigate and explain why people belong to faith communities and explain the reasons for diversity in religion

2b: evaluate the challenges and tensions of belonging to a religion and the impact of religion in the contemporary world, expressing their own ideas

3i: ethics and relationships: questions and influences that inform ethical and moral choices, including forgiveness and issues of good and evil

3j: rights and responsibilities: what religions and beliefs say about human rights and responsibilities, social justice and citizenship

PHOTO STARTER

Display the photographs of alcohol and a bookmakers. Ask students to say what these things represent. *(Alcoholic drinks and gambling.)* Ask students to express some of the different views they have heard expressed about these two things. Ask them to explain their own view. (You could make reference to current concerns over 'binge drinking' and the introduction of more gambling facilities, including 'super casinos'.) Ask students what they think a Muslim attitude to these things might be. *(They are both forbidden.)*

STARTER ACTIVITY

• **Display** the title "Home work".
• Students discuss the duties they have at home. Are they expected to:
  – keep their room tidy?
  – help with housework?
  – look after younger siblings?
• Use feedback from the pairs to discuss 'living at home' as experienced by the students.

MAIN TEACHING

• Introduce the topic and read through 'Living as a Muslim at home' with the students. Identify the main points. *(respect for elders and care of the elderly)*
• Students complete 'Over To You' (1).
• Talk about duties a Muslim child might have that would not be typical of children in families who followed another faith or none. *(For example, the requirement to undertake religious education, attending the madraseh, etc.)*
• Students read through 'Living as a Muslim at work' and complete 'Over To You' (2) and Copymaster (21). (The Copymaster asks students to consider the suitability of certain jobs for Muslims. Some are obvious while others may require qualification to assess their suitability, e.g. the holiday rep. The shift work advert is asking students to consider the effect this type of work would have on family life. Would a Muslim woman, in particular, be able to take this job and fulfil her duties to the family?)

- Work through 'Living as a Muslim in the community' with the students. Ask students to identify the main points:
  - Islam transcends race – all Muslims are part of a worldwide family.
  - Giving to the poor is a duty (this will be covered in unit 27).
  - Hospitality and sociability are encouraged. The mosque acts as a centre to encourage strong community ties.
  - There are dress codes associated with modesty.
- The dress code for women, in particular, is another area where there is great debate and sometimes controversy within the Muslim community and beyond. It has been seen by some as a restriction placed on women while others argue that it is to assist them in remaining modest and avoiding unwanted sexual attention.
- The issue of hijab – as in the general instruction to both men and women to dress 'modestly' - could be discussed, as could students' views on other more proscriptive notions of appropriate dress for Muslim women.
- In October 2006, Jack Straw, the Leader of the House of Commons, provoked a controversial debate when he made comments about asking Muslim women to remove their veils when visiting his MP surgery. Students could study the ramifications of this and organise a debate of their own.
- Students complete 'Over To You' (3).
- Read through 'Shari'ah' and 'Check It Out'.
- Students could be asked to draw two pictures: one showing an action that might be following 'the path' and one showing an action which wasn't.

PLENARY
- Students recall the main points of living in the family, in work and as part of the community.
- Students discuss the Copymaster.

Look at the advertisements for jobs below. Which ones would a Muslim not consider applying for and why? Which jobs could they apply for and what questions might they want to ask?

Butcher Required

Derwent's family butcher requires a skilled butcher to work in their city centre retail outlet. Duties include preparing meat and selling to the general public. We are a traditional butcher renowned for providing local produce to the highest standard.

Skilled Seamstresses Needed

As a busy clothing manufacturer, we are currently seeking staff to work from home in the production of quality clothing. Exceptional rates for the right people.

MODELS! MODELS! MODELS!

We are a young and exciting modelling agency. We currently require female models for an exciting new range of swimwear for a major client. Please send suitable photo and details of experience to Mandy at Box 36.

Part-time Vacancy

We currently have a vacancy for a part-time worker to share duties in our general store selling newspapers, magazines, foodstuffs and alcohol. No experience needed as training will be given.

Shift Workers Required

Local food packaging plant requires shift workers to maintain production. Good rates. All applicants must be willing to undertake all shifts on a rota basis.

Shifts are:
   6am – 2pm
   2pm – 10pm
   10pm – 6am

Holiday representatives needed to welcome guests at a number of resorts around the Mediterranean and Greek Islands. Must have excellent inter-personal skills and abilty to socialise. Work involves several weeks living abroad.

22 Teacher Notes
SAWM

NATIONAL FRAMEWORK LINKS

1a: investigate and explain the differing impacts of religious beliefs and teachings on individuals, communities and societies

1b: analyse and explain how religious beliefs and ideas are transmitted by people, texts and traditions

1h: interpret a variety of forms of religious and spiritual expression

2b: evaluate the challenges and tensions of belonging to a religion and the impact of religion in the contemporary world, expressing their own ideas

3h: expressions of spirituality: how and why human self-understanding and experiences are expressed in a variety of forms

3p: reflecting on and carefully evaluating their own beliefs and values and those of others in response to their learning in religious education, using reasoned, balanced arguments

STARTER ACTIVITY

- **Display** the title "I couldn't live without..."
- Ask students to consider everything beyond their requirements for sufficient food, water and shelter as luxuries. Given this, ask students to list the five 'luxuries' they would find it most difficult to live without.
- Students compare their five luxuries with a partner and then feed back to class.
- Students consider the statement "As long as you can afford it, you should have whatever you want."

MAIN TEACHING

- Introduce the topic and work through the material. Ask students to identify the main points and begin to construct a diagram about fasting. [See **display** file.]

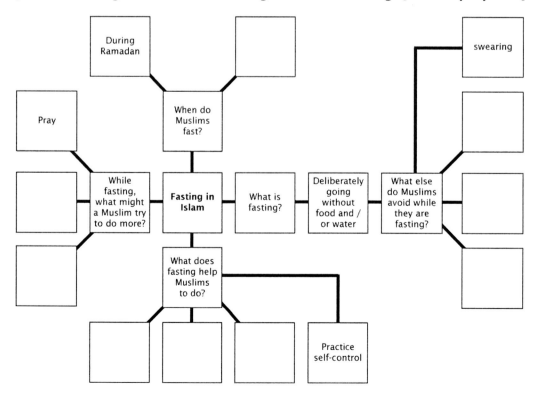

68

- Begin this diagram and then ask students to copy and continue it, working through the material in the Student Book.

> **Additional information**
> Ramadan is the ninth month of the Islamic calendar. As this calendar is based on lunar months, Ramadan occurs at different times each year. As a Pillar of Islam, sawm is an important part of Islamic worship and the month of Ramadan is viewed as being a particularly blessed and beneficial time. It is a time when Muslims seek to draw close to Allah and to distance themselves from the 'attractions of the world'. It allows Muslims to practice self-discipline, sacrifice and sympathy for those who are less fortunate. This latter comes about particularly because, during fasting, all Muslims experience hunger and deprivation, which is a daily reality for many people around the world. The fasting also helps all Muslims to feel an equality – they are all experiencing the same thing wherever they are in the world.

- Work through students' diagrams, asking what new questions and information they have added.
- Students complete 'Over To You' (1-5).
- Ask students who they think is being referred to in Extract A, which mentions fasting being prescribed for 'those before you'. *(Jews and Christians)* Students could carry out some research on fasting in other faith traditions.
- Students consider their responses to the statement in the starter activity about the rightness of having anything you can afford. Do they think the idea of fasting suggests an attitude which would disagree with the statement?

PLENARY
- Ask students to say what Muslims gain from carrying out the fast during Ramadan. (*A sense of self-discipline, closeness to God, peace, an understanding that they have performed another duty, etc.*)
- Students say what they think they might achieve from a similar fast.

23 Teacher Notes
THE MOSQUE

NATIONAL FRAMEWORK LINKS

1b: analyse and explain how religious beliefs and ideas are transmitted by people, texts and traditions

1c: investigate and explain why people belong to faith communities and explain the reasons for diversity in religion

1h: interpret a variety of forms of religious and spiritual expression

3h: expressions of spirituality: how and why human self-understanding and experiences are expressed in a variety of forms

3n: visiting, where possible, places of major religious significance and using opportunities in ICT to enhance students' understanding of religion

PHOTO STARTER

Display the picture of the minaret. Ask students what they think this might be and where it could be found. *(A tower on a mosque.)* Say that this is called a minaret. Ask students to say why the minaret is so tall. *(Possibly to allow the call to prayer to be heard over greater distances.)*

STARTER ACTIVITY

- **Display** a number of pictures of the outside of different mosques.
- Ask students to say what they think these buildings are.
- Ask students to identify any common features.
  (Some, but not all, have minarets. Some have domes.)
- Discuss the differences and why they exist.
  (different times of construction, different cultural traditions, etc)

MAIN TEACHING

- Say that all the pictures show mosques in different parts of the world.
- Read the introductory paragraph and ask students to identify the main functions of the mosque as given. *(to meet and enjoy social interaction and to prostrate oneself or pray)*
- Read through the material in 'There are mosques everywhere'.
- Look again at the pictures from the starter activity and say where they are from.
- Students can carry out research into a local mosque:

> - Where is the nearest mosque?
> - How long has it been there?
> - Is it purpose-built?
> - If not, what was the building used for previously?
>
> [a directory of mosques is available at www.mosques.co.uk]

- Students complete 'Over To You' (1-2).

- Read through 'Other uses for a mosque' and discuss how these all put the mosque at the centre of Muslim community life:
  - *A school.* Children learn Arabic so that they can read the Qur'an in its original form. They study the Qur'an in the school and learn about the faith. Family life is very important to Muslims and the family is the building block of society. Children are an important part of this structure and the means of the faith continuing into the future. Attending the school ensures the children become closely knit members of the Muslim community.
  - *A law court.* It will be important for Muslims to try to sort out difficulties that arise within the community in their own way.
  - *A location for religious celebrations.* Certain rites of passage are significant for families but also affect the wider community. A wedding or the birth of a child are signs to community members of the community being strengthened and continued. When the community wishes to celebrate a festival, the mosque provides a focal point for this, again strengthening the sense of identity for the members of the faith.
  - *A community centre.* A community often needs to come together to discuss issues that affect different members. Muslims living in a predominantly non-Muslim country will feel that a discussion in the mosque will be in the company of others who understand beliefs and values that affect responses to issues in society.
- Students complete 'Over To You' (3) and Copymaster (23). The Copymaster asks students to consider the religious significance behind the different uses of the mosque as required in 'Over To You' (3).
- Students read through 'Running water' and 'Praying on the street'.
- Students complete the 'Take Time To Think' activity or use this for a homework assignment.

PLENARY

Use questions and answers to recall the main teaching points:

- Name two external features of a purpose-built mosque. *(dome, minaret, courtyard)*
- Why do Muslim males try to pray together in a mosque as often as possible? *(Muhammad said that praying together was more beneficial.)*
- Name two other uses of a mosque besides prayer. *(school, law court, meeting place, community centre, place for religious celebrations)*

Think about all the activities that take place in a mosque. Say how each of these are different ways of Muslims expressing their spirituality. Which of their beliefs are being shown to be important in each of these activities?

24 Teacher Notes
INSIDE A MOSQUE

NATIONAL FRAMEWORK LINKS

1b: analyse and explain how religious beliefs and ideas are transmitted by people, texts and traditions

1c: investigate and explain why people belong to faith communities and explain the reasons for diversity in religion

1h: interpret a variety of forms of religious and spiritual expression

3h: expressions of spirituality: how and why human self-understanding and experiences are expressed in a variety of forms

3n: visiting, where possible, places of major religious significance and using opportunities in ICT to enhance students' understanding of religion

3g: religion and science: issues of truth, explanation, meaning and purpose

PHOTO STARTER

Display the picture of the mihrab. Ask students what they think this might be and where it could be found. (*It is an alcove found within a mosque.*) Talk about the decoration and ask if this suggests the alcove is special. (*It is special and is always placed in the mosque in a particular place.*) Say that, when you are facing the alcove, you are facing in the direction of a particular place. Ask students if they can think which place this might be (*Makkah*) and why (*it is the birthplace of Muhammad*).

STARTER ACTIVITY

- **Display** the question "What happens in places of worship?"
- Students work with a partner to think of all the uses they can for places of worship with which they are familiar through personal experience or prior learning.
- Prepare a list of the uses from students' feedback.

MAIN TEACHING

- Introduce the topic. Work through the opening paragraph and 'The prayer room', asking students to identify the main points.
- Students complete 'Over To You' (1-2).
- Students read through the information about 'The mihrab' and 'The minbar' and complete 'Over To You' (3-4).
- Students read about 'The mosque and me' and complete the 'Take Time To Think' activity.
- Students complete Copymaster (24), which asks them to highlight the beliefs and attitudes being expressed through the interior of a typical mosque.
- Students could visit a mosque to enhance their learning. If this is not possible, use pictures of the inside of a mosque which can be displayed or handed out.
- Students could use the internet to look for 'virtual tours' and other information.

A picture gallery of the Birmingham Central Mosque is available at: www.bbc.co.uk/birmingham/faith/places_of_worship/muslim/ birmingham_central_mosque.shtml

PLENARY

Students read out information from the Copymaster indicating the significance of the features mentioned. Suitable responses might be:

- *There are no pictures of animals or people because these are forbidden. Only Allah can create such things.*
- *There are no pictures of Muhammad because he did not allow these as they could lead to idolatry. Only Allah is to be worshipped.*
- *The mirhab faces Makkah because this is the birthplace of Muhammad, the most holy place in Islam.*
- *The imam is raised so that he can be heard. He is not thought to be more holy than the other people in the mosque.*
- *There is always running water because Muslims must wash before prayer.*
- *Muslims remove their shoes as a mark of respect for Allah.*
- *Carpets can be kept clean easily and the prayer hall is a sacred space. Some are marked in 'bays' so that individuals do not have to bring their own mats.*
- *Clocks show different times for prayer. Praying five times a day is one of the Pillars of Islam.*

What are the hidden messages?

Look at the picture of the inside of a mosque. Say why all the details that have been highlighted have significance. What do they teach Muslims about their faith?

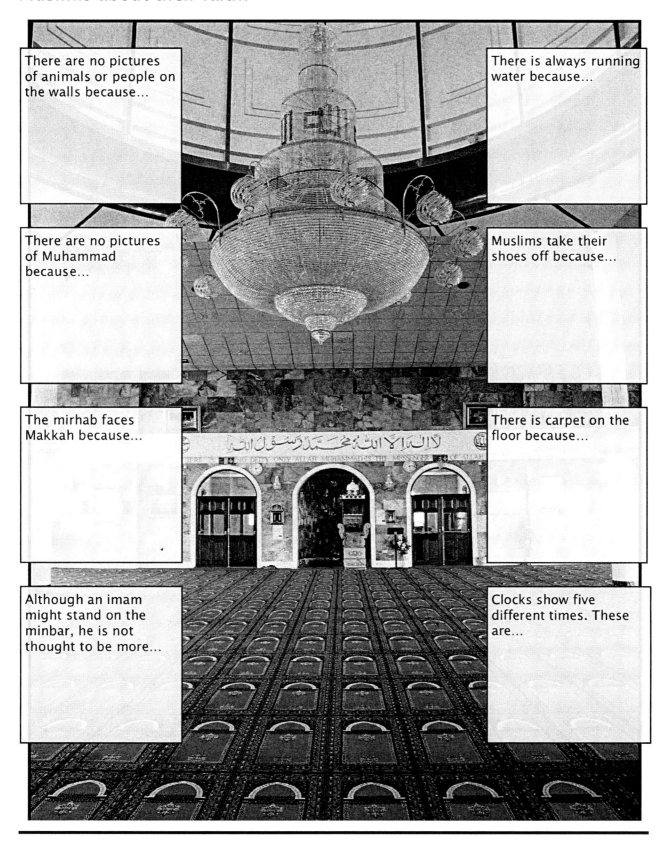

There are no pictures of animals or people on the walls because...

There is always running water because...

There are no pictures of Muhammad because...

Muslims take their shoes off because...

The mirhab faces Makkah because...

There is carpet on the floor because...

Although an imam might stand on the minbar, he is not thought to be more...

Clocks show five different times. These are...

25 Teacher Notes
MUSLIMS IN BRITAIN

PHOTO STARTER

Display the picture of the Halal food shop. Ask students if they notice anything special about the shop. *(It has the sign advertising Halal food.)* Ask students if they can think what this might be. *(It is a kind of special food which Muslims are allowed to eat.)* Ask what the significance will be for Muslims living in Britain if they can only buy and consume halal food. *(They will have to buy regulated food from approved sources only. This is particularly true of meat. They will not be able to buy meat from an ordinary butcher since it will not have been prepared in the correct way. There need to be special shops to cater for the needs of the Muslim community.)*

STARTER ACTIVITY

- **Display** the title "On the move".
- Ask students to work in groups to produce a list of reasons that people have for moving to and living in a country other than the one in which they were born.
- Students consider difficulties that might be experienced by people who choose to do this.
- Take feedback from the groups and produce a list of the different reasons.

MAIN TEACHING

- Introduce the topic.
- Analyse the list of reasons from the starter activity and see which, if any, might apply to Muslims moving to this country.
- There will be many different reasons for this:
  - Some will have travelled here because conditions in their home country would not allow them to achieve all they might.
  - Some come to train or to gain qualifications.
  - Some come to work in fields such as medicine.
  - Some may come to join family that are already resident here.
  - Some may be refugees – for example, many people were driven out of Uganda by Idi Amin in the 1970s.
- Consider the difficulties people may have when moving to another country.
  (For example, different language, different customs, different food, different standards, etc.)

- Point out that people have to make adjustments whenever they move between countries and cultures. People who move to continental Europe have to learn a new language and get used to new laws, customs and routines. People who move from the UK to an Islamic country often have to learn a new language and also have to adjust to different rules and expectations of behaviour in public.
- This sets the context for considering the particular difficulties that can be faced by Muslims living in Britain and for discussion on the issues raised.
- Throughout, it will be necessary to be sensitive to Muslim students in your class. The work does allow for them to express their opinion and to say 'how it really is' for them. The work is a good opportunity to promote greater understanding.
- Read the introductory paragraph, which mentions the fact that Muslims have been living in the UK for at least 200 years. Say that there are many Muslims who have not moved here but have been born here.
- Underline the point that some of the difficulties faced are not due to the fact that people have moved to a different culture but rather that followers of Islam lead a distinctive lifestyle.
- Work through the material on possible difficulties in 'Medical services'.

Additional information

A further issue facing female Muslims training or working in medicine is the issue of wearing the veil. In October 2006, Birmingham University School of Medicine banned the wearing of the veil in a move that was intended to 'help aid good communications' between medical students, their colleagues and patients. A Muslim MP, whose constituency is in Birmingham, stated that everybody's safety and security needed to be considered. He stated that removal of the veil was acceptable where professional issues were concerned, when doctors and nurses meet with patients, for example.

- When reading 'Time to pray', ask students to consider what this means for an employer. How might adjustments be made to accommodate a Muslim's requirement to pray during working hours?
- Considering the issue of 'Dress', students can consider the idea of 'separateness' as well as some of the practical difficulties presented by the dress code.
- The issue of 'Boy/girl relationships' is relevant to all young people. This provides the opportunity to discuss students' views on the matter in general. They can then consider the particular problems faced by Muslim young people. Remind students of the tradition of arranged marriages in Islam. Remind them too that there is a range of attitudes to various aspects of the faith. Some Muslim families are very traditional while others are more liberal or 'modern'.
- Muslim students can talk about their experiences and thoughts.
- Students can use the internet to find further information about Muslims in Britain. A useful site is for Islam Awareness week [www.iaw.org.uk], which includes a virtual classroom which details some of the contributions made by Muslims in history.
- Students complete 'Over To You' (4-5) and consider the question from 'Take Time To Think'.

PLENARY
- Students outline their understanding of the idea of integrating into a different society.
- They mention certain difficulties Muslims might have with integrating into UK society.

THE 'HAVES' AND THE 'HAVE-NOTS'

NATIONAL FRAMEWORK LINKS

1a: investigate and explain the differing impacts of religious beliefs and teachings on individuals, communities and societies

1e: discuss and evaluate how religious beliefs and teachings inform answers to ultimate questions and ethical issues

2b: evaluate the challenges and tensions of belonging to a religion and the impact of religion in the contemporary world, expressing their own ideas

2d: reflect and evaluate their own and others' beliefs about world issues such as peace and conflict, wealth and poverty and the importance of the environment, communicating their own ideas

3j: rights and responsibilities: what religions and beliefs say about human rights and responsibilities, social justice and citizenship

3k: global issues: what religions and beliefs say about health, wealth, war, animal rights and the environment

STARTER ACTIVITY

Give out copies of the statements from Resource sheet (26) or **display** these. Students discuss each statement and how far they agree or disagree with each.

MAIN TEACHING

• Introduce the topic and read through the introductory material. This paints a picture of the world with which the students may be familiar: the poor 'south' and the rich 'north'. Students may be familiar with other terms which indicate this division, such as the 'developed' and 'developing' world.

• Although, in global terms, absolute poverty is concentrated in the south, it is important to recognise that relative poverty and associated deprivation exists in the countries of the north. In the UK, over a quarter of people live in low income households where they suffer from worse health, lower life-expectancy, lower levels of participation in society and lower life chances than those from more affluent households.

• Many religions have the care of the poor as a top priority and, when these teachings were given, there would not have been the global perspective that we now have. The teaching would have been about showing a concern for the poor within the community.

• This is still true today – the poor are within our local community as well as the global community of which we are now far more aware.

• Talk about human rights as enshrined in the United Nations Declaration.

• Put students into small groups to discuss 'Over To You' (1). Take feedback from the groups and ask for situations which might produce 'want' or 'fear', where the students think these might be experienced most keenly in the world, and who might have the most responsibility for seeing that these things are eradicated.

• Read through 'Islam, wealth and poverty' with the students.

• Students carry out 'Over To You' (2). (This asks for research into the situation regarding widows and orphans. These people were particularly vulnerable. An orphan may have inherited property before 'coming of age' and older relatives could have attempted to steal this directly or to make use of it for their own ends. Widows were left without a man to earn a living and act as 'provider'.)

- Read through 'Sharing with those in need'. Students discuss what could be meant by spending wealth in "Allah's way" and what might be meant by the picture of grain multiplying.
- Students respond to the questions in 'Take Time To Think'. This could be carried out in pairs or small groups. Part of the tax paid by those in employment in this country is used to provide income support for poorer families. When the government gives 'aid' to foreign countries, where does the money come from? Do the students think that individuals still have a responsibility to act on behalf of the poor even though there are these government initiatives? *(Hopefully, yes. There is such a huge disparity between the rich and the poor. Also, government initiatives often fail to provide sufficient cover for every eventuality – charities have to be established to provide shelters for the homeless, for example. Globally, governments are obviously unable to address the issues satisfactorily – there still need to be relief agencies operating around the world funded by charitable donations.)*

PLENARY

Students recall the main teaching points of the lesson:
- To suggest possible causes of poverty or contributing factors. (Lack of education, lack of skills, over population of an area, limited natural resources, unequal distribution of resources, etc.)
- To suggest why the inequality in the world, as suggested in the unit, continues. (Greed, selfishness, lack of love, etc.)
- To give examples of how the Muslim teachings would have an impact on this situation.

The modern world would not be possible without money.

Money makes people selfish.

If people learnt to share then everybody would have enough.

If you are lucky enough to be rich then you should share what you have.

We only need food, warmth and shelter. Anything beyond that is a luxury.

Money causes more problems than it solves.

27 Teacher Notes
ZAKAH AND SADAQAH

NATIONAL FRAMEWORK LINKS

1a: investigate and explain the differing impacts of religious beliefs and teachings on individuals, communities and societies

1e: discuss and evaluate how religious beliefs and teachings inform answers to ultimate questions and ethical issues

2b: evaluate the challenges and tensions of belonging to a religion and the impact of religion in the contemporary world, expressing their own ideas

2d: reflect and evaluate their own and others' beliefs about world issues such as peace and conflict, wealth and poverty and the importance of the environment, communicating their own ideas

3j: rights and responsibilities: what religions and beliefs say about human rights and responsibilities, social justice and citizenship

3k: global issues: what religions and beliefs say about health, wealth, war, animal rights and the environment

STARTER ACTIVITY

- **Display** the statement "The world's poor need a hand up not just a hand out."
- Ask students to discuss what this statement means and how it might be achieved. (*'The poor' need help in an immediate crisis situation to obtain life's essentials such as food, water and shelter. They also need assistance in moving towards greater self-sufficiency. For example, buying fair trade goods promotes sustainable employment and education possibilities. In the UK, homeless people can sell* The Big Issue *as a means of raising their own income. In both cases, the result is that people need less direct giving.*)
- Talk about the need for direct giving because some of the situations for the world's poor are so difficult and so entrenched. (*For example, continuing droughts in certain African countries which result in crop failure and the threat of starvation. Not all the homeless people in the UK can sell* The Big Issue.)

MAIN TEACHING

- Introduce the topic and read the first paragraph. Ask students to identify the main points:
  - An Islamic society should be fair and equal.
  - A duty of Muslims is to give to the poor. It is one of the Pillars of Islam.
  - Zakah means 'to purify'. Muslims see the need to be purified of selfishness and a love of money.
  - Muhammad was an orphan. The Qur'an states that Allah helped Muhammad when he was an orphan and so Muslims should help orphans and others in need.
- Students complete 'Over To You' (1).
- Read through 'Paying zakah' and 'Zakah is a blessing'. The first considers the 'mechanics' of paying zakah, the second deals with some of the spiritual and social aspects. Help students to identify the main points from these paragraphs. Point out that Islam is a complete code for living which inevitably includes economic aspects of life. Zakah is a basic principle of an Islamic economy which has social welfare and the fair distribution of wealth at its centre.

81

- Those receiving zakah are not viewed as receiving charity. Allah determines who will be wealthy and who will not. He has determined that those with wealth should give zakah. This is the means by which the poor receive what is rightfully theirs – it is Allah's provision for them. Any wealth is not viewed as belonging to a person. It has been provided by Allah for a person to use in the correct way.
- Students complete 'Over To You' (2).
- Read about 'Sadaqah'. Say that the Qur'an encourages Muslims to give these voluntary contributions to the poor and the needy and for other social welfare purposes.
- Students complete Copymaster (27).

PLENARY

- Students read out responses to the Copymaster.
- Ask students to recall any points about zakah not mentioned in this feedback.

Fill in the speech bubbles with what each person might say. Remember to mention what each does, why they do it and how they feel about it.

I have more than I need because...

Since I have wealth, I...

Allah has chosen to give me a hard life but...

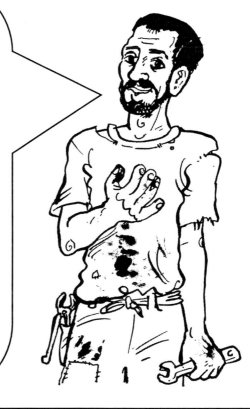

28 Teacher Notes
ISLAMIC RELIEF WORLDWIDE

NATIONAL FRAMEWORK LINKS

1a: investigate and explain the differing impacts of religious beliefs and teachings on individuals, communities and societies

1e: discuss and evaluate how religious beliefs and teachings inform answers to ultimate questions and ethical issues

2b: evaluate the challenges and tensions of belonging to a religion and the impact of religion in the contemporary world, expressing their own ideas

2d: reflect and evaluate their own and others' beliefs about world issues such as peace and conflict, wealth and poverty and the importance of the environment, communicating their own ideas

3j: rights and responsibilities: what religions and beliefs say about human rights and responsibilities, social justice and citizenship

3k: global issues: what religions and beliefs say about health, wealth, war, animal rights and the environment

PHOTO STARTER

Display the picture of the children. Ask the students what they think an appropriate response to the kind of situation these children represent would be. *(to try to help)* Ask students what they think a Muslim response would be. *(to seek to change the children's lives for the better)*

STARTER ACTIVITY

- **Display** the words from Resource sheet (28) or make them up as cards and distribute.
- Put the students into small groups and allocate one of the problems on the cards. The group should spend 2-3 minutes discussing the implications of their problem: how or why the problem occurs, what physically happens, what is the immediate result, what might be the long-term results, how people can respond.
- Each group gives a brief feedback to produce a 'snapshot' of major world problems and disasters.

MAIN TEACHING

- Say that the starter activity provides the backdrop for this work which looks at how one Islamic organisation responds to the types of situation discussed.
- Read through the introductory paragraphs and add any further insights to the points made by the students in the starter.
- Read through 'Islamic Relief Worldwide' and 'Check It Out' with the students.
- Students complete 'Over To You' (1-4).
- Read about 'Caring for orphans'. Explain that the care of orphans is a theme that keeps appearing in the Qur'an. Muhammad's own experience of being an orphan gave him an insight into how difficult it can be.

- Talk about the number of orphans there are. It is sometimes difficult to imagine the scale of the problem from the viewpoint of the United Kingdom. Students may be aware of HIV/AIDS. This disease is killing millions of people and leaving many millions of children as orphans. There are many other reasons why there are many orphans in many countries around the world, usually in the 'developing world'. These include war, drought, poverty and disease.
- Students could research Islamic relief organisations on the internet and use Copymaster (28) to record their findings. [e.g. www.islamic-relief.com, www.islamicaid.org.uk]

PLENARY

- Students identify the types of situations Islamic Relief Worldwide seeks to address.
- Students say why Muslims would believe that they should support such an organisation.

WAR	FLOOD
FAMINE	EARTHQHAKE
DROUGHT	DISEASE
NO SAFE WATER	LACK OF EDUCATION

CHARITY RESEARCH RECORD

Name of charity

History of charity

Aim of charity

Scope of work

Examples of projects

Beliefs that guide charity

Teacher Notes
CREATION AND PARADISE

NATIONAL FRAMEWORK LINKS

1b: analyse and explain how religious beliefs and ideas are transmitted by people, texts and traditions

1d: analyse and compare the evidence and arguments used when considering issues of truth in religion and philosophy

1e: discuss and evaluate how religious beliefs and teachings inform answers to ultimate questions and ethical issues

1g: interpret and evaluate a range of sources, texts and authorities, from a variety of contexts

2b: evaluate the challenges and tensions of belonging to a religion and the impact of religion in the contemporary world, expressing their own ideas

2e: express their own beliefs and ideas, using a variety of forms of expression

3e: beliefs and concepts: the key ideas and questions of meaning in religions and beliefs, including issues related to God, truth, the world, human life and life after death

PHOTO STARTER

Display the picture of the person digging. Talk about the idea of people creating gardens and tending the ground. What do the students feel is the appeal for people in creating and tending gardens and growing flowers, fruit and vegetables? (Some people find gardening therapeutic, others enjoy creating somewhere beautiful where they can relax. Some say it 'puts them in touch with nature'. People enjoy growing flowers to look at and some say fruit and vegetables from the garden are the freshest and tastiest.) Ask about 'tending the ground' in the wider sense; that is 'looking after the world'. What do the students feel about a sense of duty towards doing that?

STARTER ACTIVITY

- **Display** a picture that shows a 'wonder of nature'. For example, an intricately formed flower, a brightly feathered bird or a montage of an acorn and an oak tree.
- Ask students for their responses to the image.
- Ask how a believer from a theistic religion (a person who believes in God) might 'see' God in this image. *(For example, in the beauty of nature, the suggestion of purpose, order and design or the 'miracle' of an oak tree 'coming out of' an acorn.)*
- Explain that Muslims believe that Allah created the world and so they can 'see' God in the natural world.

MAIN TEACHING

- Read through the introductory paragraph and identify the points from Extract A with the students. God:
  - created the heavens and the Earth in six days
  - established authority over creation
  - established 'laws' to do with 'cosmology' - night following day; the sun, moon and stars having their set movements
  - cherishes (loves) the world
  - sustains (upholds) the world

- Students read through the 'Check It Out' section and complete 'Over To You' (1-2).
- Read through 'On the Day of Judgement'.
- Discuss the elements of mutual responsibility and collective responsibility that are mentioned.
    - Human beings are the most important part of creation. Every Muslim must care for every part of creation. Therefore Muslims should care for other human beings.
    - Muslims should share resources properly because Allah has provided enough for everyone.
    - Each Muslim will be questioned about how they have treated Allah's creation on the Day of Judgement.
- Read about 'Sin in Paradise'. Discuss the images of a perfect world being spoiled. What do students think about the image of human beings not being satisfied, even though they had 'everything they could possibly need'? Is there any evidence of this today?
- Read 'Who was Iblis'. Ask students how Iblis might test the faith of Muslim believers.
- Students complete 'Over To You' (3).

PLENARY

Students recall the Muslim understanding of how the universe and the Earth came into existence.

30 Teacher Notes
STEWARDS OF CREATION

NATIONAL FRAMEWORK LINKS

1a: investigate and explain the differing impacts of religious beliefs and teachings on individuals, communities and societies

1b: analyse and explain how religious beliefs and ideas are transmitted by people, texts and traditions

2a: reflect on the relationship between beliefs, teachings and ultimate questions, communicating their own ideas and using reasoned arguments

2d: reflect and evaluate their own and others' beliefs about world issues such as peace and conflict, wealth and poverty and the importance of the environment, communicating their own ideas

3k: global issues: what religions and beliefs say about health, wealth, war, animal rights and the environment

STARTER ACTIVITY

- **Display** the title "Out of balance".
- Students work in pairs to discuss an aspect of the natural world that they feel is 'out of balance', such as the loss of rainforests, the increase in pollution, the increase in 'greenhouse' gases, 'desertification' (increasing amounts of land turning to desert due to over-grazing or over-cultivation).
- Collect students' feedback to the class to present a picture of some of the difficulties facing the planet. Ask the students to identify the causes of the issues they have discussed. *(human activity)*

MAIN TEACHING

- Introduce the topic and read the 'Check It Out' material, which outlines the extent of God's creation as understood by Muslims.
- Read through 'Human beings and creation'.
- Use questions and answers to establish that the ideas are understood:
  - Why are human beings regarded as the most important part of Allah's creation? *(because they alone can worship Allah)*
  - What are human beings expected to do? *(look after Allah's creation)*
  - Why does the Muslim community have a special responsibility? *(because they have received Allah's true revelation in the Qur'an)*
  - What will all human beings have to give account for? *(how they have treated Allah's creation)*
- Students read 'The whole of creation hangs together' and complete 'Over To You' (1-2).
- Read through 'The example of Muhammad'. From this and Extract C, students list the things Muslims can learn from Muhammad's example:
  - Care is due to all living creatures.
  - Avoid waste.
  - Care for the Earth.
  - Working to grow food for people or animals is worthwhile.
- Students complete Copymaster (30).

PLENARY

- Students feed back ideas from the Copymaster.

Look at these images and describe how a Muslim might react to what is happening.

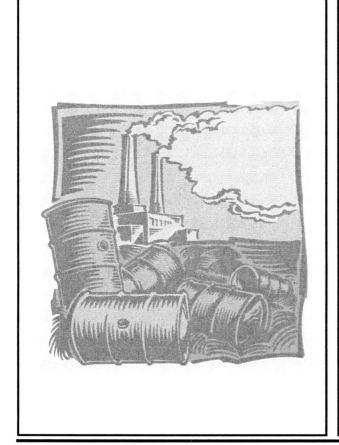

THE MUSLIM ATTITUDE TO ANIMALS

NATIONAL FRAMEWORK LINKS

1a: investigate and explain the differing impacts of religious beliefs and teachings on individuals, communities and societies

1b: analyse and explain how religious beliefs and ideas are transmitted by people, texts and traditions

2a: reflect on the relationship between beliefs, teachings and ultimate questions, communicating their own ideas and using reasoned arguments

2d: reflect and evaluate their own and others' beliefs about world issues such as peace and conflict, wealth and poverty and the importance of the environment, communicating their own ideas

3k: global issues: what religions and beliefs say about health, wealth, war, animal rights and the environment

STARTER ACTIVITY

Display or distribute the statements on Resource sheet (31). Students discuss these statements in pairs or small groups. Are there any statements on which they all agree?

MAIN TEACHING

- Introduce the topic and read through 'Muslims and animals'. Students identify and record the main points:
  - All animals are part of Allah's creation.
  - Human beings are the most important part of Allah's creation.
  - Dominance (control) over animals is granted.
  - Dominance does not give permission for cruelty.
  - Any cruelty to an animal will be punished by Allah.
  - Animals can be killed for food but not for sport.
- Read through 'Experiments on animals [vivisection]'.
- Talk about how this issue is comparatively recent in terms of human beings and their relationship with animals. Medical understanding and practice has moved on rapidly. Testing the effects of cosmetics is also a fairly recent phenomenon. Neither would have been applicable to the society in which the teachings of Islam arose. However, the principles and practices do hold, since there are clear stipulations about cruelty to animals.
- Students consider the thoughts of some Muslims regarding these issues and complete 'Over To You' (1).
- Read about 'Ihram'. Students may have prior knowledge of the Hajj and the celebration of Eid-ul-Adha. [See **Additional resources** below.]
- Students complete 'Over To You' (2) and the 'Take Time To Think' exercise.

Additional information

Eid-ul-Adha is a time where Muslims remember Ibrahim and his commitment to Allah. This serves to remind them of their own total commitment to Allah. Ibrahim was ready to sacrifice his own son to prove that he was willing to give total obedience to Allah. Because Allah saw that Ibrahim was willing to obey, he provided a ram for sacrifice instead. The festival has most significance for those on the Hajj but it is celebrated by all Muslims in the world at the same time as a mark of unity. There is obviously a high demand for animals at this time. The central part of the festival is the choosing of an animal for slaughter. Permitted animals include a sheep, cow, goat or camel. Traditionally, the father, as head of the family, would slaughter the animal himself. This is not allowed in the UK and the animals are sent to an approved (Halal) slaughter house. There are strict rules for the slaughter of animals which are intended to ensure that the animals feel no unnecessary pain or fear.

Regarding food laws, there is no prohibition on eating meat, so Muslims are not required to be vegetarian. It is acceptable to kill animals for food. There are restrictions on the types of meat and animals that can be eaten. Halal (allowed) meats are obtained from sheep, goats, cows, camels, chickens. Meats that are not allowed (haran) are pork, carnivorous animals, animals with fangs (e.g. lions), birds of prey, amphibians (e.g. frogs) and almost all reptiles.

Regarding eating meat and vegetarianism, a Muslim would dispute that killing animals for food is cruel and an infringement of animal rights. By arguing that animals have similar rights to those of humans, people are putting both on the same level. This opposes the Muslim view which sees human beings as superior in the hierarchy of creation. The argument would also be that animals should have responsibilities and duties if they are to be accorded rights. They should be held accountable if they infringe the rights of other animals. It would be illogical to say that it is wrong for a human to kill a sheep in order to eat but acceptable for a lion to do the same.

A counter argument could be that human beings, perhaps because they are superior, have a choice and the killing of animals for them is a more deliberate choice than for a lion or other predatory creature.

PLENARY

Students feed back using their spider diagram from 'Over To You' (2) to recap the main points about Muslim attitudes to animals.

Animals are not the same as human beings and should not have the same rights.	Animals are there for human beings to use for their benefit.
Because animals are defenceless, they should be protected by human beings.	If animals are used by human beings, they should be looked after properly.
People who are deliberately cruel to animals should be punished by law.	Human beings have always hunted animals for food – it is perfectly natural.
All of life is sacred and nobody has the right to cause the end of a life.	Vegetables are living things – it is wrong to eat a carrot.

32 Teacher Notes
THE JIHAD

NATIONAL FRAMEWORK LINKS

1a: investigate and explain the differing impacts of religious beliefs and teachings on individuals, communities and societies

1b: analyse and explain how religious beliefs and ideas are transmitted by people, texts and traditions

1e: discuss and evaluate how religious beliefs and teachings inform answers to ultimate questions and ethical issues

2c: express insights into the significance and value of religion and other world views on human relationships personally, locally and globally

3i: ethics and relationships: questions and influences that inform ethical and moral choices, including forgiveness and issues of good and evil

3j: rights and responsibilities: what religions and beliefs say about human rights and responsibilities, social justice and citizenship

3k: global issues: what religions and beliefs say about health, wealth, war, animal rights and the environment

3l: interfaith dialogue: a study of relationships, conflicts and collaboration within and between religions and beliefs

STARTER ACTIVITY

• **Display** the title "Fight for freedom".

• Talk briefly about substances such as nicotine or alcohol and how people can become addicted to these. There is a point at which a person's body craves the substance even though another part of them knows it is harmful and that they would like to stop smoking or drinking. Pose the questions 'Who is in control?' and 'Are these people really free?'

• Students discuss in pairs any things they can think of that have some level of 'control' over them. (Can they go without watching a favourite TV soap opera?) Is there any habit or behaviour that they feel they have to struggle with?

• Take feedback.

MAIN TEACHING

• Introduce the topic and say how this concerns the Muslim concept of struggle.

• Read through the introductory paragraph.

Additional information

Muhammad began his teaching in Makkah and, although this was mainly religious, there were also implied criticisms of the attitudes and customs of some of the wealthy members of the population. Certain rich merchants approached him with an offer of marriage into a wealthy family and a large share in local trade. Muhammad refused both and, as a result, found himself facing hostility from the people of Makkah. It is difficult to establish how much of the persecution and turmoil that followed is purely religious. There are other factors such as tribal loyalties, political considerations and economic interests.

- Read through 'A holy war' and the associated 'Check It Out' material.

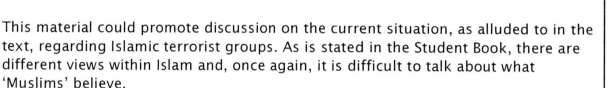
- Read through 'Fighting injustice' and the quotes from the young Muslims. Remind students of the starter activity, which explored the notion that human beings are often struggling with conflicting desires and emotions. Students can refer to this when considering 'Over To You' (1).
- Students complete 'Over To You' (2-3).

PLENARY
Students explain the significance of the 'Greater Jihad' and how each Muslim is involved.

33 Teacher Notes
ISLAM AND SCIENCE

NATIONAL FRAMEWORK LINKS

1a: investigate and explain the differing impacts of religious beliefs and teachings on individuals, communities and societies

1b: analyse and explain how religious beliefs and ideas are transmitted by people, texts and traditions

1e: discuss and evaluate how religious beliefs and teachings inform answers to ultimate questions and ethical issues

2c: express insights into the significance and value of religion and other world views on human relationships personally, locally and globally

3i: ethics and relationships: questions and influences that inform ethical and moral choices, including forgiveness and issues of good and evil

3j: rights and responsibilities: what religions and beliefs say about human rights and responsibilities, social justice and citizenship

3k: global issues: what religions and beliefs say about health, wealth, war, animal rights and the environment

3l: interfaith dialogue: a study of relationships, conflicts and collaboration within and between religions and beliefs

PHOTO STARTER

Display the photograph of the view. Ask students what it makes them think about.

STARTER ACTIVITY

- **Display** the question "Which came first, the chicken or the egg?"
- Students work in pairs or small groups to discuss this conundrum.
- Take feedback and discuss some of the ideas and issues raised.

MAIN TEACHING

- Read through the introductory paragraph, 'Signs of Allah in the universe' and 'Check It Out'.
- Say that the material points out that the Qur'an:
  - constantly encourages people to reflect on and understand the world;
  - also says that, if people do this with faith, they will be able to see signs of Allah in the world he has made.
- There is no need for a conflict between science and Islam, provided any evidence produced by science is taken as a sign of Allah's providence.
- Lead students in a discussion about their perceptions of the world. Do they:
  - see evidence for a creator in the natural world?
  - feel uplifted when they see spectacular views?
  - feel in awe of the sea when it is stormy?
  - feel calmed by the gentle waves lapping on a beach?
  - feel grateful for all the beauty in the world?
  - feel amazed at the intricacy of life?
  - experience some of these things but don't see that it has anything to do with God?
- Read about 'Islam and the origin of the universe'.

97

- Talk about the 'Big Bang' theory, which is one explanation put forward by science as the means of the universe beginning. Point out that this almost inevitably leads some people to ask the question, 'What caused the 'Big Bang'?' Muslims who consider the theory of the 'Big Bang' to be reasonable would argue that Allah is the cause of it. Students can discuss their own views, remembering that all should be respectful of other people's ideas and beliefs.
- Read about 'Islam and the theory of evolution'. Talk about the difficulties presented by evolution for those who take a literal reading of the creation stories. The material suggests that there are similarities between the Jewish / Christian accounts of creation and that found in the Qur'an. Each mentions days of creation with certain aspects of the universe and the world being created on different days.
- Regarding the creation of human beings, the Qur'an states that:

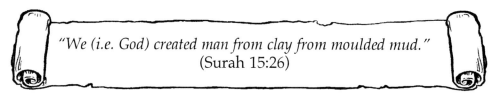

"We (i.e. God) created man from clay from moulded mud."
(Surah 15:26)

- Point out that there are people from the 'Creation' faiths of Judaism, Christianity and Islam who are able to embrace some ideas from evolution. However, the difference, and possible area for conflict, lies with the understanding of what 'drives' the evolutionary process. For secular humanists, evolution is an entirely natural process with no initial cause and no 'guiding hand'. The changes that have taken place over millions of years are the results of natural adaptations to environmental conditions or 'accidental' mutations. For believers in a creator, including Muslims, the idea would be that evolution is a mechanism instigated and guided by God.
- Remind students that there are a range of understandings within the Muslim faith and traditions. Some would not countenance the idea of evolution, for example. Reinforce the fact that it is difficult to say 'all Muslims believe...' on every issue. They all, obviously, believe in Allah as creator. The differences in this area emerge when considering how He created and what it means for Him to be 'reproducing' creation, as suggested in the Student Book.
- Students complete 'Over To You' (1-2) and Copymaster (33).

PLENARY

Students use their responses to the Copymaster to recall:
- what all Muslims believe about the creation of the world
  (that Allah is the Creator of everything)
- what some Muslims believe about the creation of the world
  (that there was a 'Big Bang' but that Allah instigated this)
- what all Muslims believe about human beings
  (that they are created by Allah)
- what some Muslims believe about evolution
  (that it is the mechanism used by Allah to produce life as we know it today, including human life)

The origins of the universe and the Earth

What all Muslims believe

What some Muslims believe

What I beleive

Human life and evolution

What all Muslims believe

What some Muslims believe

What I beleive

ASSESSMENT

1) a) What are the similarities that Muslims say exist between Islam, Christianity and Judaism?

   b) What are the elements that distinguish Islam from Christianity and Judaism?

   c) What are the possible reasons for these differences?

   (Units 1, 2, 32, 33)

   Similarities
   Muslims refer to Christians and Jews as 'people of the book', referring to Jewish scripture and the Christian New Testament.
   Muslims recognise a common heritage in Abraham (Ibrahim).
   Muslims consider other people from Jewish scripture (Noah and Moses) and from Christianity (Jesus) as prophets.

   Differences
   Islam teaches that Jews and Christians have distorted and corrupted the words of God given in their writings.
   Islam holds Muhammad to be the greatest and last of Allah's prophets.
   Muslims do not believe that Jesus is the Son of God since this takes away from their idea of the oneness of God.

   Level 4
   Students will be able to describe some links and differences.

   Level 5
   Students will understand that similarities and differences illustrate distinctive beliefs and suggest possible reasons for these differences.

   Level 6
   Students use religious and philosophical vocabulary to explain reasons for diversity.

2) Give a brief understanding of Allah from a Muslim point of view. Say what Allah has done and how Muslims should behave towards him. (Units 4, 5, 6)

   Allah is the creator of the universe. He made all things and he made all human beings. Everything that happens is the will of Allah and people who are Muslim give themselves over to the will of Allah.

   Level 4
   Students use a developing religious vocabulary to describe Muslim beliefs about Allah.

   Level 5
   Students use an increasingly wide religious vocabulary to describe Muslim beliefs about Allah and the impact these beliefs have on the lives of Muslims.

   Level 6
   Students use religious and philosophical vocabulary to give an informed account of Muslim beliefs about Allah and how these beliefs affect their lives.

3) Write about the Shahadah and how it has an impact on people's lives. (Unit 6)

Shahadah – the statement of faith.

Level 4
Students say that when people can recite this and mean it in their hearts then they are a true Muslim. It is the first thing a new-born hears and the thing that Muslims hope is the last thing on their lips when they die. Life is based on this statement of faith.

Level 5
Students say why people belong to a religion and why Muslims follow Islam. They can say what the statement of faith means and how it affects the lives of Muslims.

Level 6
Students can express the impact of the faith of Muslims in Allah and of submission to His will on their lives. They describe how these beliefs affect the actions and practices of Muslims. They identify the statement of faith as something which all Muslims adhere to even if there are other differences about belief and interpretation regarding some other aspects of the faith, such as the role of women, for example.

4) Write about Salah – prayers. (Units 7, 8)

Level 4
Muslims are called to pray five times a day. Praying five times a day is part of the discipline that needs to be shown. It indicates that people are putting duty to Allah above all other things. Muslims carry out ritual washing, called wudu, before they pray. They should pray facing Makkah because this is the birthplace of Muhammad.

Level 5
There are set prayers which are accompanied by set actions. These are called rak'ahs. Muslims can also pray their own prayers which are called du'a prayers.

Level 6
Prayers remind Muslims that Allah is central to everything they do. Muhammad likened prayer to washing one's body in a stream – it is about purifying the body and the soul and being clean in the presence of Allah.

5) Write about Sawm – fasting. (Unit 22)

Level 4
Muslims have to fast during the month of Ramadan. This is the tenth month of the Islamic calendar. They have to go without food or drink from dawn to dusk. This helps them to be disciplined and to remember people who are not as fortunate as they are.

Level 5
During fasting, Muslims are reminded that all good things come from Allah. They are undergoing a discipline in which they are denying their body what it craves. It is important that they are able to control their body and their physical desires to show that they are committed to Allah. Fasting helps to bring the family and the community together.

Level 6
During the fast of Ramadan, Muslims try to live by even higher standards than usual. They will try to spend more time reading the Qur'an and have their thoughts more firmly on Allah. They refrain from sexual relations, from anger and from harsh words. During this time, Muslims are seeking a higher level of spiritual purity. Fasting brings all Muslims to the same level – there is an increased sense of all Muslims being equal and of all belonging to the worldwide Muslim community, the 'Ummah'. At the end of Ramadan is the festival of Eid-ul-Fitr.

6) Write about Zakah. (Units 10, 27)

Level 4
All Muslims have to give a portion of their money to the poor. This is to make sure that the poor are looked after. The portion is 2.5% of money available after a person's family and personal needs have been provided for.

Level 5
Islam teaches that Allah wants the world to be just and fair. All people are equal in the eyes of Allah but it His will to make some people wealthy while others are poor. It is the duty of those whom Allah has made wealthy to look after the needs of those who are poor.

Level 6
Muslims understand that zakah is a duty but it is also a spiritual blessing. It is an act which helps to purify actions and thoughts. Muslims believe that all things belong to Allah and so wealth and money should not be hoarded or only used selfishly. Muslims remember that all actions will be taken into account by Allah on the day of Judgement. A right attitude to the poor and needy is therefore seen as a fundamental part of living the proper way.

7) Write about the Hajj. (Units 5, 9, 31)

Level 4
All Muslims who are able to must go on the Hajj once in their lifetime. The Hajj is a pilgrimage to Makkah and Medinah, the two most important and sacred sites in Islam. During the Hajj, Muslims wear special clothes (white robes). This is partly a sign of purity but it also suggests the idea of equality between Muslims. Since everyone is wearing the same kind of thing, there is no outward indication of wealth or poverty or social status.

Level 5
Students will show that undertaking the Hajj is demanding. It is a form of expression about commitment to Allah and to the family of Muslims. People benefit from travelling, praying and being with fellow believers.

Level 6
At the end of the Hajj is the Feast of Sacrifice (Eid-ul-Adha), which remembers Ibrahim and his willingness to sacrifice his son. Meat from slaughtered animals is shared with the poor. This shows that all people should be included in the festivities, even if they cannot afford to put their own animals up for slaughter. This underlines the beliefs that all are equal in the eyes of Allah and that people whom Allah has blessed with money should take care of the poor. Everyone is part of the Muslim family.

8) Describe some groups of which you are a part and how this gives you a sense of belonging and say how this compares to the experiences that a Muslim might have. (Units 3, 14, 21)

Level 4
Students identify groups to which they belong. They may mention family, school, clubs and sports teams. There may be some outward signs of belonging to such groups (uniform or sports kit). Students may identify having shared goals or intentions. Students will identify some groups to which Muslims belong (the family, the community, the 'Ummah' or worldwide community). They mention guidance on clothing that may be indications of belonging to the Islamic community.

Level 5
Students mention the strength gained from a feeling of unity within a group. Muslim clothing guidelines are discussed in terms of their significance regarding 'modesty'.

Level 6
Students give insights into their own understanding of the question of identity and belonging. They can explain how these things are understood from a Muslim point of view. They mention some of the challenges that some people can face if they are part of a smaller group within society. They might make parallels between the experiences of a 'special interest' group in school and some of the challenges of belonging to a religious group in the modern world, with particular reference to Muslims.

9) Explain what happens in a Muslim family and why the family is so important. What are other views about the role of the family in today's society?
(Units 15, 16)

Level 4
Students describe some of the duties and responsibilities of different members of a Muslim family. They explain that the family is such an important thing for Muslims because it is the foundation of Muslim society. It is where people learn about their faith and about how to behave properly towards one another.

Level 5
Students mention the extended family as a common structure in Muslim societies. They discuss some of the benefits of an extended family and some of the possible disadvantages. They compare the views expressed by other people in society from different faiths or none.

Level 6
Students provide a detailed outline of Muslim family life. They are able to say how certain beliefs are expressed through the family and the duties and responsibilities members have. They compare a range of views on the family from different standpoints.

10) Discuss the traditional role of women in Islam, how this is changing in some areas and your own thoughts about a woman's role in society.
(Units 15, 17, 19, 21, 25)

Level 4
Students describe some of the traditional roles and duties of women in Islam such as creating a home and bringing up children. They describe some of the guidance about clothing for women. They suggest some possible origins for these traditional roles and the notion of dressing 'modestly' and describe ways in which these are changing. They can apply their own ideas to these beliefs and practices.

Level 5
Students say why men and women in Islam have definite roles and responsibilities. They discuss the role of the Qur'an in providing guidance for people's roles and behaviour. They discuss the different guidance for women's clothing and the fact that they are not allowed to lead men in prayer. They recognise that some Muslims adhere more strictly to these roles and guidelines than others. They explain their own position on the role of women in society and their views on the Muslim understanding.

Level 6
Students mention the Qur'an and the Hadith as the sources of authority on the role of men and women in Islam. They discuss the different interpretations and understandings regarding the clothing worn by women in Muslim society. They discuss the issue of women being allowed to pray in a mosque and the apparent segregation of men and women which occurs in some mosques. They give insights into the situation from their own point of view and can refer to some of these issues as challenges facing Muslims in the contemporary world.

11) Discuss poverty in the world and Islam's response. (Units 5, 26, 27, 28)

Level 4
Students will describe some situations locally and in other parts of the world where people are poor. They provide some reasons for this. They identify the Muslim duty to look after the poor and say that it is a teaching from the Qur'an. They describe how individual Muslims contribute to the poor through paying zakah and also through donating to organisations such as Islamic Relief Worldwide.

Level 5
Students use increasingly religious language to describe the impact of certain teachings on people's beliefs and therefore on their actions. They explain Muslims' duty to look after the poor in terms of Allah's desire for the world to be just and fair, the fact that all human beings have equal value in the eyes of Allah and their desire to please Allah. They mention a number of ways in which the poor of a local community might be helped (through the sharing of meat at Eid-ul-Adha for example) and organisations that respond to global poverty.

Level 6
Students use religious and philosophical vocabulary to give an informed account of the Islamic understanding of wealth and poverty and of teachings relating to this. They mention that all things happen because of the will of Allah, so some are destined to have wealth while others are destined to be poor. It is the religious duty of those with wealth to care for those who are poor. They mention and analyse some teachings from the Qur'an and the Hadith which form the basis for these ideas and beliefs. They describe the situation as a challenge for people living in affluent, modern societies.

12) Discuss the relationship between Islam and science with particular reference to the origins of the Earth, evolution and the use of animals in medical research (vivisection). (Units 29, 30, 31, 33)

Level 4
Students outline 'The Big Bang' and Allah's creation as two different accounts of the beginning of the world. They explain how some Muslims accept 'The Big Bang' but only as a result of Allah's actions. Students discuss the theory of evolution and how views on this differ within the Muslim community. They explain how some Muslims can accept evolution. Students discuss the fact that all of life is sacred as far as Muslims are concerned because everything was made by and belongs to Allah. Only he has the right to begin life and to end it. However, Muslims understand that human beings are more precious than animals and so they would accept that vivisection is necessary as long as no unnecessary pain is caused to the animals.

Level 5
Students describe 'The Big Bang' and Allah's creation and identify them as two accounts for the beginning of the world. Students explain that there is a range of interpretations regarding the relationship between these two accounts. They say how some Muslims can accept 'The Big Bang' as an act of Allah while others adhere to the literal interpretation of the creation account in the Qur'an. Students explain the way in which some Muslims are able to accept the idea of evolution but only in terms of a mechanism used by Allah to create and develop life, not as a purely natural, random process. Students indicate the hierarchy of creation which places human beings as the most important part of Allah's creation and therefore within their rights when it comes to making use of animals. The rights of the animals, as part of Allah's creation, must also be protected.

Level 6
Students give informed accounts of the Islamic beliefs about the beginning of the world and the theory of evolution and explain some reasons for the diversity of belief regarding these within the Islamic community. They are able to discuss the hierarchy of creation, explaining that human beings are the most important part of creation but also have the highest degree of responsibility. They can explain the Muslim justification for making use of animals in scientific experiments for medical research and compare this to their own views.

Badger Publishing Limited
15 Wedgwood Gate
Pin Green Industrial Estate
Stevenage, Hertfordshire SG1 4SU
Telephone: 01438 356907
Fax: 01438 747015
www.badger-publishing.co.uk
enquiries@badger-publishing.co.uk

Badger KS3 Religious Education
Muslim Beliefs and Issues
Teacher Guide with CD-Rom

First published 2007
ISBN 978-1-84691-103-3

Text © Pat Lunt 2007
Complete work © Badger Publishing Limited 2007

Acknowledgements
Photos © Alex Keene, The Walking Camera, with the following exceptions:

Teacher Book: 23 Couple (3) © Corbis.

CD Display Files: 12 (2), 29 (2) © Paul Martin Digital; 23 (2) © Adam Wilmott.

Publisher: David Jamieson
Editor: Paul Martin
Designer: Adam Wilmott
Illustrator: Juliet Breese
Cover photo: Alex Keene, The Walking Camera

Printed in the UK